CHRIST IN THE DRAMA

CHRIST IN THE DRAMA

A Study of the Influence of Christ on the Drama of England and America. The Shaffer Lectures of Northwestern University, 1946

BY

FRED EASTMAN

Essay Index Reprint Series

BOOKS FOR LIBRARIES PRESS
FREEPORT, NEW YORK

Library of Congress Cataloging in Publication Data

Eastman, Fred, 1886–
    Christ in the drama.

    (The Shaffer lectures of Northwestern University,
1946) (Essay index reprint series)
    1. Jesus Christ in literature. 2. English
drama--History and criticism. 3. American drama
--History and criticism. I. Title. II. Series:
Northwestern University, Evanston, Ill. Shaffer
lectures, 1946.
[BT555.E3 1972]   822'.009   79-167336
ISBN 0-8369-2647-1

PRINTED IN THE UNITED STATES OF AMERICA
BY
NEW WORLD BOOK MANUFACTURING CO., INC.
HALLANDALE, FLORIDA 33009

To

RICHARD and ARTHUR

Introduction: The Criteria for This Study

A TOUGH-MINDED reader, on seeing the title of this book, will probably wish to fire a volley of questions. Is the author going to try to prove that Christ has had a wide influence on the drama of England and America? How does he propose to show it? What criteria will he use? Will he count the number of quotations from Christ? Or cite the miracles performed in his name? Or weigh the Christian preachments in the mouths of the characters? And why limit the consideration to England and America? It may be well to answer such questions before we go further.

I do not propose to prove that Christ's influence on the drama of England and America has been wide. In fact, I do not attempt to prove anything. This book simply records an effort to *discover* the influence of Christ in representative dramas of these two countries. That he has had some influence no one will deny. Every culture known to man has produced drama. In practically every instance it has risen out of religious rites and has reflected in its spiritual and ethical content the religion in which it originated. Thus the representative dramas which have evolved in Buddhistic, Mohammedan, and other cultures bear the imprint of the founders of those faiths. The same could be said of their music, art, literature. Occidental cultures in which Christianity has been the dominant religion are no exception. This is not to say that *every* drama created in a given culture reflects the influence of its dominant religion; far from it. For in every culture there has always been at least

vii

one other religion quite antithetical to the dominant one. It is
some form of secularism: the worship of material things—
money, power, pleasure, prestige. Many dramatists have reflected only this worldly religion in their plays. My concern is
not with them but with those dramas which probe more deeply
into the struggles of the human soul.

How discover the influence of Christ in such dramas? How
avoid the pitfalls of propaganda, sentimentality, and preach-
ment? These questions I pondered long and did not see my
way clearly until Aeschylus and Shakespeare took me in hand
and tutored me in their strange visitation reported in Chapter I. Thereafter the light began to break upon my path. It was
obvious from the beginning, however, that one could not discover the influence of Christ by counting the number of quotations from him, or by parading the plays that have centered
around ministers and priests and nuns, or plays in which
husband and wife are reconciled by the prayers of a devout
child. There was surely a better way and one which even the
most sternly critical reader would approve. After Aeschylus
and Shakespeare had given me their warnings and outlined the
development of the drama as an art (and how could one study
the influence of Christ on any art without understanding
something of that art's history and technique and peculiar
genius?) it came to me. It was this: I could arrive at an
appraisal of the influence of Christ on a drama by an *examination of three essential factors: (1) the principal characters,
their motivations and reactions; (2) the author's spiritual insight; and (3) the effect of the play as a whole upon the audience.* A brief consideration of these will reveal their importance.

First, the principal characters. How does a dramatist go
about his art of revealing a character's spiritual insides? He

thrusts him into the midst of some vital conflict that mounts episode by episode to a crisis. In that crisis the dramatist brings heavy pressures to bear upon the character's mind and heart. These pressures become so intense that the character's very soul is broken open. There in that riven soul the audience sees his innermost affections and loyalties, his values and motives, his hopes and fears. In that crisis the character must make some great choice between two or more solutions to the conflict—a choice which will determine his actions for better or worse. Choice is character in action. Aristotle held that the action of the great Greek tragedies flowed inevitably from the choices of the characters. But back of the choice is the character's standard of values, his highest loyalty, his deepest affection. These are the spiritual elements a playwright reveals when, in the supreme crisis of the play, he breaks open a character's soul. A man's real religion is shown in the choices he makes in the crises of his life. An examination of a character in a drama at the moment when he makes his choice between good and evil, or—more often—between lesser good and higher good, discloses in some measure whether his values, his loyalties, and his affections have been influenced by the life and teaching of Christ.

Second, the author's spiritual insight. If, in the play as a whole, he demonstrates an understanding and insight concerning the spiritual life in harmony with the understanding and insight of Christ is it not fitting to give credit to the Galilean?

Third, the total effect of the play upon the audience. Some plays leave the audience depressed although they have been written and acted with the skill of expert craftsmen. In the 1930's a man on leaving a theatre where he had seen a powerful play by Eugene O'Neill remarked, "It's so good to get out into the Depression again!" Other plays send the audience away exalted in spirit and with a deepened sense of fellowship with God and man. The plays may not mention God or Christ or religion. They may deal with material that seems sordid. But the playwright has discovered something eternally true and beautiful blooming in the muck. *It is not the material, not the background, not even the plot—but the total result of the author's insight and his handling of the material that produces the final effect.* Peter and John were once thrown in prison on suspicion of being Christians. Their persecutors had no particular evidence against them, but the record reads, "When they saw the *boldness* of Peter and John" they knew that they had been with Jesus. Just so, some plays convince by their *effect* that those who made them have been with him whether they knew it or not.

By these criteria, varying and combining them to avoid monotony, I have examined the plays of the leading playwrights of England and America and selected representative ones for treatment here. It would have been quite possible to double or triple the number without going beyond the dramatists of England and America, and to have multiplied it further by including some of the works of the great German, French, Norwegian, and Russian writers. The limits of my available time and the reader's patience precluded this. Moreover it seemed better to consider a comparatively few plays intensively than many sketchily. For the reader who would like to consider other plays of a similar nature I have appended a list which may prove suggestive.

FRED EASTMAN

Acknowledgments

GRATEFULLY I acknowledge my indebtedness to the following who have helped to bring this volume to completion:

Professor Charles S. Braden and his colleagues of the Faculty of Northwestern University who invited me to deliver the John C. Shaffer Lectures in the Spring of 1946. This lectureship, founded in 1923, is designed to "promote an appreciation of the life, character, and teachings of Jesus." Within these broad limits I had full freedom to develop the subject in any way that seemed interesting. The present work is an expansion of the four lectures I delivered in response to this invitation.

My wife who has given intelligent criticism at each stage of the book's progress, and has patiently read galley and page proof to catch the errors I had missed.

Mrs. Martha Hutchins, my secretary, who has typed the manuscript and checked many a date and spelling.

My friends and colleagues, President A. C. McGiffert, Jr. and Professor Amos N. Wilder of The Chicago Theological Seminary, who have made constructive suggestions concerning various chapters.

Miss Ellen Shippen of the Macmillan Company who has encouraged me with kindly editorial counsel.

The publishers of the plays discussed for their cooperation in granting permission to make the specific quotations mentioned in the footnotes.

F. E.

CONTENTS

CHRIST IN THE DRAMA

CHAPTER I

The Drama Before Shakespeare

SUDDENLY, late one evening in the midst of preparing these lectures, I became aware that I was not alone. There in my study, peering at me over the stacks of books and plays on my desk, stood three spectres. Two of them I recognized: the one in the white Grecian robe was surely Aeschylus, the great soldier, poet, composer, and founder of Greek drama; the other in Elizabethan court garb under a short cape could be none other than Shakespeare. The third, in a modern business suit, standing to one side with a sneer upon his face, I could not name although I had a vague sense of having seen him on Times Square. None of them made any motion to speak; they simply stared at me and their eyes seemed to gaze through me as easily as I could see through their spectral bodies. What to do? After all, it was my study and at least two of these men were distinguished beyond any visitors I had ever entertained. Clearly it behooved me to make them welcome.

"Good evening, gentlemen," I said nervously. "You honor my poor workshop. Won't you sit down?" Hastily I removed the books from three chairs, but the three continued to stand. I went back to my desk, faced them, and again tried to break the ice. "Is there anything I can do for you?" No answer.

A happy thought seized me. "Or have you by chance come to help me? Heaven knows I shall be grateful for assistance.

You see, I am beginning an essay on Christ and the Drama. Your visit is most timely. Others have written on the subject but none has had the advice of such able artists. If you would be willing to counsel me it might give my treatment a bit of an edge——"

The third spectre—the unknown—interrupted with a rude laugh. "Save your breath, Professor," he said. "I don't know about these others, but I haven't come to help you in any such nonsense. I've come to warn you."

"Warn me?" I exclaimed, nonplussed. "Of what?"

"Of the whole idea. You'd better drop it; it's too hot to handle."

"I'm not afraid of it," I replied. "But why should you trouble yourself to warn me? In fact, I haven't the privilege of knowing you, have I?"

"That's part of your danger," he said. "My name is Lucre. I am the Executive Secretary of the Association of Theatre Owners, Past, Present, and Future."

"Indeed! Then you ought to be in position to know a great deal about the drama."

"I am. I know what it's for."

"And that is?"

"To make money for theatre owners."

"That," I agreed, "is doubtless one of its functions, and a necessary one in most instances. But——"

"No 'buts,' " he interrupted. "And nothing else. Especially no religion. Whenever religion gets mixed up with drama there's hell to pay. We lose money."

"Not always, by any means," I countered. "There have been many instances of definitely religious dramas that made substantial profits."

"Only exceptions that prove the rule," he insisted. "Religion's got no place in the theatre."

Here was a chance to bring Aeschylus into the discussion. But could he speak English? He might well have learned it if he had lived in the spirit world all these centuries and maintained his original eagerness of mind. There was an easy way to find out. I turned hopefully to him with a question, "How about that?"

"I must disagree with Mr. Lucre," he answered.

"I knew you would," I said, grateful not only that he spoke English but that he avoided hexameters, probably in deference to my own pedestrian prose. "Your own majestic tragedies are deeply religious. Your *Oresteia* and *Prometheus Bound*——"

Mr. Lucre interrupted again. "And who ever made a penny out of them?" he demanded. "The State had to support them. I can prove from the records that Greece spent more money on those plays and similar ones than it spent on its national defense. If it had spent more on its army and navy and less on such stuff it wouldn't have been conquered by its enemies."

Aeschylus drew himself up with dignity. "The decline of the power of Greece began not in her army and navy but in the spirit of the people themselves. That was not in the days of the tragedies of Sophocles and Euripides and myself, but centuries afterward when the people turned from using their drama to *interpret* life to using it to *escape* from life."

Mr. Lucre fairly snorted. "You fellows always have an alibi," he exclaimed, "but the fact remains no one ever made money out of your plays. And it's money that keeps the theatres open."

"If that is all that keeps them open perhaps it would be better to close them," replied Aeschylus.

"And if they close where will the dramatists be?" Mr. Lucre queried angrily. "Where will they put on their plays? Answer me that."

"Easily," said Aeschylus, smiling. "They will produce them in the places they used before the theatre came into existence—on hillsides under the open sky, around camp fires, on village greens, and in the temples of religion."

"Amateur stuff!" sneered Mr. Lucre.

"Yes, amateur in the strictest sense—done for the love of it."

"Nonsense!" cried Mr. Lucre. "You can't put on dramas without a stage with scenery and lights and other equipment."

I had wanted to bring my third visitor into the debate and this seemed the cue. "How about that, Mr. Shakespeare?" I asked.

"I managed to get along without them," he answered.

Mr. Lucre raged. "I might have known it was useless to talk sense to a professor and a couple of authors. I'll not waste more time on you now. But mark my words: you're running into danger if you get drama mixed up with religion. Whenever that's happened it's meant trouble for theatre owners. We won't stand for any interference with our business. You try it and you'll wish you hadn't." And with this terse admonition he 'disappeared himself.'

Relieved, I turned hopefully to my nobler visitors. "And now, gentlemen," I began, "may we get down to the more pleasant business of your call? I am right, am I not, in assuming that you have come to help me think through this task?"

To my surprise and disappointment they shook their heads.

Aeschylus spoke first. "I am afraid not," he said. "We, too, have come to warn you of the dangers in the subject you have undertaken."

My heart sank. If these masters of the drama who had probed the depths of men's souls in their plays would not help me, who would? But I must learn what dangers they saw in the subject. Perhaps in the process I could beguile them into giving me something constructive.

"What are the dangers you see?" I inquired humbly.

"Mr. Shakespeare and I are not in entire agreement. If he will permit me I shall tell you what dangers I see and then turn you over to him."

Shakespeare nodded. "Have at him," he said, "and damned be he who first cries Hold, enough! I'll be looking over these books the professor has assembled. Never saw so many tomes on drama. Maybe I can learn something." Whereupon he turned his back upon us, selected a book, and sat down. I tried in vain to glimpse the title of the book, hoping it would not be the one containing Tolstoi's critical essay on Shakespeare. However, the chance seemed small and my concern gave way to relief that the Bard, evidently on a poet's holiday from pentameters, was speaking in matter-of-fact prose.

Aeschylus began his attack. "I warn you," he said, "against confusing the *influence* of Christ upon the drama with the *exploitation* that the Christian Church has made of drama to propagate its own dogmas."

"I see this danger," I replied, "and I shall beware of it. But did you not use your own dramas to further the worship of your god Dionysus?"

"That I did not!" he exclaimed emphatically. "Teachers of drama, and even historions, who did not understand what I was doing, have often accused me of it. But is not true. The orthodox religion of Greece in my day was fatalistic. Greeks believed that all of life was predestined by the Fates over which men had no control. The early parts of my plays reflect that prevailing belief of my people, just as Shakespeare's plays often reflect the beliefs of his audiences in witches and fairies. But before I finished I made it clear that each character's destiny was determined not by something outside, but something *inside* himself. That was the essence of 'tragic fallacy'—that the cause of the hero's downfall was in some weakness in his own character."

"Shakespeare had the same insight in his tragedies, did he not?" I asked.

"He got it from the Greeks," replied Aeschylus shortly.

Shakespeare smiled rather sourly over his shoulder. "I've been told that Bacon wrote my plays. Seems to have been the Greeks instead."

Aeschylus ignored him and continued. "You see, I respected the orthodox religion, but I did not make my dramas subservient to it. Had I done so they would have perished with the religion of that day."

"Would you have every dramatist a heretic?" I inquired.

"No. But I would have him free."

"Free from what—and for what?"

"Free from the requirement of conformity to the dictates or dogmas of any religion. Free for an honest interpretation of life as he sees it."

"Of course," I agreed, "but a dramatist can't interpret life in a vacuum. He must use the insights of his own philosophy and religion."

"True. He will acquire his insights wherever he can. I am

only contending that he should not exploit the drama to promote any religion. When he does so he makes his theme, not his characters, dominate his play. He pushes his characters about like pawns on a chessboard to win the game for his religion. He prostitutes his art. Religion and drama are sister arts. Neither should seek to be master of the other, and neither should consent to be servant."

"Your warning is well taken," I said. "I shall strive to discriminate between religion contributing a spiritual insight and religion using drama to promote its own dogmas."

"In that case," he said with a sigh of relief, "there may be some hope for your essay."

"Your enthusiasm exhilarates me," I remarked dryly.

"There is another danger," he continued, ignoring my churlishness. "It concerns your audience. It may be thinking of drama only as a means of entertainment and be unaware of its origin in the Greek religious festivals and its development as an art through which the deepest struggles of the soul could be interpreted."

I assured him that my audience was much too intelligent to conceive of drama only as amusement. And I insisted that if I took time to trace the origin and development of drama as an art there would be no time left for my main subject.

"It can be done," he said, "especially with the aid of a new art which we who dwell beyond the River Styx have learned from some recent arrivals from the motion picture world."

"Where can I see a demonstration of this new art?" I inquired.

"Sit where you are," he replied, "and I shall demonstrate it to you. You will see as much history of the drama in a few minutes as your books can give you in a hundred pages."

"But where is the machine and where is the operator?"

Aeschylus laughed. "In the spirit world," he said, "we are blessed with freedom from machines of the kind you know. My mind is the machine, my memory the picture, and I am the operator. I shall drape a fold of my white robe over my arm to make the screen. Then I shall project the pictures from this side of the robe; you will see them from your side. That is all there is to it."

"Wouldn't Shakespeare like to see it?"

Shakespeare yawned. "Thanks. I've seen it. Besides, I have one of my own for you. Meanwhile I'd like to finish reading what this fellow Tolstoi says about me. Seems he doesn't like my plays. I should have stuck to sonnets."

Aeschylus began his demonstration. How can I describe it? It was not an ordinary motion picture—a flat projection upon a screen. It had three dimensions—depth as well as height and breadth. It combined the qualities of television and stereoscope so that it gave me the sense not only of witnessing the scenes but of participating in them. The bright colors of Greece, the sharp outlines of mountains, the white foam of the sea, the purple vineyards, the glorious Acropolis and Parthenon, the Temple of Dionysus—these were but the background against which unfolded the story of the development of drama from its primitive origins to the magnificent achievements of Aeschylus and Sophocles and Euripides in the Golden Age.

I saw first the aborigines dancing their stories of the hunt, a chorus of women urging the actors on to greater effort. Then the early agricultural tribes dancing and acting out their prayers for rain and sun and for bounteous harvests. A century or two later—a minute or two on the robe of Aeschylus—I was sitting beside a watchfire listening to Homer sing his tales of ancient heroes and of the gods who dwelt on Mount Olympus and occasionally tangled themselves in the affairs of men. The scenes leaped another era and on a spring day I was in the great outdoor Temple of Dionysus at Athens watching the drama emerge out of the religious rituals—the choruses and dances—in honor of that great god of fruition and vegetation.

Step by step Aeschylus showed me how as the decades passed the proportion of music and dancing in these festivals declined while the proportion of story and dialogue and drama increased. First one actor was introduced, then another, and another. The more the drama grew in effectiveness the larger grew the crowds until some 20,000 people were in attendance. By this time the festivals had taken the form of dramatic contests in which the leading poets of Greece competed. Aeschylus emphasized the fact that any dramatist, to win a contest, must catch and hold the interest of these huge crowds and make his play more effective in its emotional power than the plays of his competitors.

In the fire of this competition the poet-playwrights discovered that certain factors of human interest were essential for every play. These factors, Aeschylus explained, were Story, Characterization, Conflict, Suspense, Choice, Climax, Solution, Theme, and Emotion. Each playwright wove these elements into his plays in his own way—but he left any of them out at the peril of losing the contest. The combined effect of these elements—when skillfully woven together—was to produce in the audience a catharsis of the emotions. That is, it aroused and cleansed the emotions so that the people went away with their spirits refreshed, their hearts exalted, and their imaginations aflame.

I asked him to show me how he had worked out this dramatic pattern in his own trilogy of plays—the *Oresteia*. He did so, and when the third play had been completed I saw the great audience leave the temple-theatre in that state of spiritual exaltation. They had seen not only a powerful story— they had seen new light on an old struggle and gained a new insight on the ancient problem of crime and its punishment, sin and its forgiveness. Whether they knew it or not, they had seen ethics in the making. Aeschylus had breathed into their old religion a new revelation of the redemptive power of suffering. Yet nowhere had he preached this new doctrine. He had shown it in action.

I tried to say something to this effect when he had finished his demonstration. I stumbled in my expression but he was quick to catch the drift of my thought.

"Yes," he said eagerly. "Action. Remember that the word drama means deeds, or acts. If you are going to show the influence of religion on the characters of a drama, you must show it in action, not in preaching. And now my mission is done and I turn you over to Mr. Shakespeare." And without waiting for my thanks he vanished.

I turned to Shakespeare only to find that he had gone to sleep! Tiptoeing to the chair in which he sat, I looked over his shoulder at the sentence of Tolstoi's essay on which his finger rested. It read, "The basic inner reason for the fame of Shakespeare has been and still is the fact that his dramas . . . satisfied the irreligious and immoral disposition of the people of the upper classes of our world." I sighed heavily and he awoke with a start.

"Sorry to disturb you," I apologized. "You must have needed a little sleep 'to knit up the ravelled sleave of care' after reading Tolstoi's essay."

He yawned, stretched, and rose. "I did," he said. "That man ravelled more than my sleeve. I must look him up and have a bout with him after I've finished with you. What's become of Aeschylus?"

"He's gone. He helped me a great deal. I hope you will be as useful to me."

"Not I. I never tried to help anyone."

"But you came to warn me of something. That would be at least a negative kind of help."

"So I did. But not to help you. It's the religious part of your subject I'm concerned about."

"What harm in that?"

"Whenever I hear religion connected with the drama I think what Christianity did to me and to other dramatists of my time. . . . Listen to this; it is a hand bill advertising the first production of *Othello* in Newport, Rhode Island, in 1761." He pulled from his pocket a worn sheet of paper and read:

PLAY BILL OF OTHELLO IN 1761

King's Arms Tavern, Newport, Rhode Island. On Monday, June 10, at the Public Room of the above Inn, will be delivered a series of MORAL DIALOGUES, in Five Parts, Depicting the Evil Effects of Jealousy & other Bad Passions, and Proving that Happiness can only Spring from the Pursuit of Virtue. Mr. Douglass will represent a noble & magnificent Moor named Othello, who loves a young lady named Desdemona, and after he has married her, harbors (as in too many cases) the dreadful passion of Jealousy. . . .

Mr. Allyn will depict the character of a specious villain, in the regiment of Othello, who is so base as to hate his commander on mere suspicion, and to impose on his best friend. Of such characters it is to be feared, there are thousands in the world. . . .

Mrs. Morris will represent a young and virtuous wife, who being wrongfully suspected, gets smothered (in an adjoining room) by her husband.

Various other dialogues, too numerous to mention here, will be delivered at night, all adapted to the improvement of the mind and manners. The whole will be repeated Wednesday and Saturday. Tickets, six shillings each, to be had within. Commencement at seven, conclusion at half-past ten, in order that every spectator may go home at a sober hour and reflect upon what he has seen before he retires to rest.[1]

"There! Not once did it mention the author, nor use the word drama. It called *Othello* a 'series of moral dialogues in five parts.' That's what Christianity did to the drama."

"O come!" I protested. "You can't blame Christianity— and certainly not its founder—for all the mistakes of Puritanism. And besides, didn't the Puritans have some justification for their feeling about the theatre?"

"Perhaps they did. But why should they punish me for all the mistakes of the theatre?"

I laughed. "Was the punishment so great? After all, they did produce your plays. Is that all you've got against Christianity in its relation to drama?"

"There is more—much more. And that brings me to the show I promised you when Aeschylus was giving his. Can you stand a double feature?"

"Ordinarily not, but in this case with relish. On with the play!"

He took his white cape from his shoulders and began to drape it over his arm.

[1] Quoted by permission from *The Romance of the American Theatre* by Mary Caroline Crawford. Little, Brown, 1925.

"You are going to begin where he left off?" I asked.

"No. I'll assume that you know how drama declined in Greece during the fourth and third centuries B.C. and never gained a place of great importance in the Roman Empire."

"Yes," I said. "And after Christianity got started in Rome I believe one of the favorite forms of amusement in the Roman theatre was the burning of Christians?"

"I don't like to think of that," he answered rather glumly.

"The Christians didn't like it either," I rejoined.

"They had a grievance," he admitted, "but when they came to power in the third century did they apply Christian principles to the theatre? Did they seek to transform it from within, cleanse it, encourage the good? They did not. They applied only repression. One of their first official acts was to outlaw the theatre and to deprive all actors of citizenship."

"They didn't know any better," I argued lamely. "At any rate, it was Christianity that gave the drama a rebirth in Europe, was it not?"

"Only after eight hundred years of repression!" he exclaimed hotly. "Think of how the art and the artists might have developed in that time had they been given the freedom that Christianity talks about!"

"But they had lost their freedom by abusing it," I maintained.

"Am I to be answered with platitudes?" he challenged. "My point is that Christianity has eight centuries of repression to repent of."

This debate was getting us nowhere but into a temper. I tried a new tack. "Very well," I said gently. "Let's agree on that. Please remember that I do not propose to defend Christianity, but only to deal objectively with the influence of its founder."

"That's better," he conceded. "And it brings me to the second point of my warning. I can best make it clear by the same new art that Aeschylus used." Thereupon he raised his cape between us and began to show upon it the story of Christianity's revival of the drama.

Now Medieval England with its green fields and hedge rows, its flocks of grazing sheep, its village centered around the church, formed the background. Again because of the three-dimensional pictures in natural color I felt myself not an observer but a participant as I joined a small crowd entering the church on Good Friday. The priest was permitted to use only Latin in the reading of the mass, but the people did not understand Latin, nor could most of them read or write any language. So the priest, eager to make intelligible the meaning of the service, resorted to a simple form of drama. At the conclusion of the mass he took the crucifix from the altar and placed it underneath while the choir sang a miserere. Then for three days there was mourning in the church. On Easter Sunday the priest took the crucifix from its sepulchre and placed it again upon the altar while the choir sang alleluias. Even the most illiterate could get the idea that the church was trying to tell them the story of a man who had been crucified, then buried as if dead, then—somehow—he had been resurrected, victorious over death. Here was a story translated into the language of action, understandable, dramatic. They wanted more.

Centuries passed in a montage that showed the development of the drama from that simple beginning through ever larger projects. The visit of the Three Marys to the Tomb and other stories of passion week followed one another. Still the people wanted more. So the priests and the choirs dramatized the birth of Jesus, the visit of the shepherds and the wise men, the flight into Egypt, the massacre of the innocents, the journey to Jerusalem, the temptations in the wilderness, the transfiguration, the parables, and on through more elaborate scenes of the betrayal, the trial before Pilate, the crucifixion, the resurrection, the descent into hell, the ascension, and the final Judgment.

Then followed episodes from the lives of the Saints. And still the people wanted more. So the priests went back into the Old Testament and dramatized naïvely the creation of the world, the story of Adam and Eve, Cain and Abel, Noah and the Ark, Abraham, Isaac and Jacob, Moses and Aaron, and the prophecies of the coming of Christ. Finally, not as a development but as an offshoot—almost an anti-climax—they dramatized their sermons in a series of Morality Plays.

In all this development certain significant changes took place in form, in content, and in spirit. The earliest plays, those of the passion, had been presented briefly and simply in the chancel with only the clergy and the choir as actors. (Sometimes the part of God was sung by three members of the choir, a bass, a baritone and a tenor, to represent the Trinity). But as the plays grew in scope and drew larger crowds they left the chancel and were presented in the nave and then upon a platform in the doorway of the church with the people standing outdoors. Here the plays were presented by laymen's guilds, each guild coming in time to sponsor the production of the story most pertinent to its own craft. Thus the masons' guild presented the story of the creation, the shipwrights' guild the story of Noah and the Ark. The stage itself became a huge platform with two stories, the upper for the action, the lower for dressing rooms. At one side of the stage stood the pearly gates of heaven, at the other side the flaming jaws of hell. At the close of each play the good characters went to heaven; the bad characters—always more numerous—went into the flaming jaws, prodded along by a host of devils. It was all very simple.

At about this phase of the story Shakespeare digressed. He said he couldn't resist showing me the stage directions for a Norman French play of the twelfth century on Adam. I quote them:

Let Paradise be set up in a somewhat lofty place; let there be put about it curtains and silken hangings, at such an height that those persons who shall be in Paradise can be seen from the shoulders upward; let there be planted there sweet-smelling flowers and foliage; let divers trees be therein, and fruits hanging upon them, so that it may seem a most delectable place. . . .

And let Adam himself be well instructed when he shall make his answers, lest in answering he be either too swift or too slow. Let not only Adam, but all the persons, be so instructed that they shall speak composedly and shall use such gestures as become the matter whereof they are speaking; and in uttering the verses, let them neither add a syllable nor take away, but let them pro-nounce all clearly; and let those things that are to be said be said in their due order.[2]

After this digression the picture proceeded. Someone thought up the idea of putting the stage upon wheels and

[2] Quoted from *Adam, a Religious Play of the Twelfth Century.* Translated from the Norman French and Latin into English verse by Edward Noble Stone. University of Washington Press, 1928. Used by permission.

rolling it away from the church so that the plays could be seen at various parts of the cities. Thus originated the term pageant which means "rolling platform." This led naturally to the next development: each guild came to have its own wagon for its own plays. So a crowd, standing on a street corner or in the marketplace, saw a series of wagons each presenting one or two scenes from the Old Testament or New. Certain communities took pride in developing a complete cycle of plays from the creation of the world to the final Judgment—a cycle consisting of from twenty-five to forty-two plays. So in the fifteenth and sixteenth centuries the York, the Towneley, the Chester, and the Coventry Cycles became famous. It took the better part of a week for one of these cycles to complete its series. Tradesmen, seeing the crowds assemble day after day, took advantage of their opportunity and established booths for selling their wares, so that the atmosphere became more and more one of a county fair—no longer a service of worship or of religious education but a festivity.

By this time the clergy had dropped entirely out of the scenes and the chief parts were played by traveling groups of minstrels and troubadours. These actors, sensing the festive mood of crowds, played down the tragic features and played up the comic. They introduced more and more secular folklore and invented characters whose sole purpose was to amuse. They gave Noah a wife with a shrewish tongue—a wife who caused him more trouble than all the animals on the Ark. In the shepherd play they introduced a stealer of sheep and gave more attention to him than to the angels who announced the birth of Christ.

Now came a new and significant phase. Some astute innkeeper, probably an ancestor of Mr. Lucre, who knew that crowds get thirsty, built next to his inn a permanent stage and invited the traveling players to present their plays upon it. He would give them free board and lodging. They would no longer have to worry about their wagons getting stuck in the deep mud of English streets in springtime. There would be seats for the well-to-do and other comforts for both audience and actors. The temptation was too strong to be resisted. By the end of the sixteenth century the itinerant wagons had practically disappeared. Permanent stages with covered galleries, most of them adjoining inns, dotted London and the banks of the Thames. The theatre was born.

A profound change in the spirit and content of the plays accompanied this physical transition. The further the plays journeyed from the church, the more they lost their sense of mission to the human spirit. In the church they had been concerned with the revelation of God to man, with sin and salvation. By the time they reached the inn-yard little thought of this had survived. The crowds at the inns wanted to laugh, not to think. So the actors gave them what they wanted. The religious elements declined and vanished; the secular, and often the vulgar, ascended.

Meanwhile a great change was taking place in the English cultural background. The national spirit had received a tremendous impetus with the defeat of the Spanish Armada and the resulting hope of English domination of the Western World. Henry VIII broke with the papacy. Young writers began to feel that they were no longer shackled by ecclesiasticism. Free spirits exulted in their freedom, but many mistook freedom for license. Elizabeth ascended the throne and befriended the budding dramatists. Then followed half a century of magnificent development of the professional drama. Morality plays gave place to Interludes and Court Plays and they in turn to early tragi-comedies, true comedies, neo-classic tragedies, chronicle plays, and tragedies. These were the glorious years of Marlowe, Ben Jonson and Shakespeare.

But Elizabeth was succeeded by James I and he by Charles I. Their corrupt courts debased the theatre and increased the resentment of the Puritans who began to turn their ire upon those dramatists who were using their freedom for license. Such playwrights, encouraged by Mr. Lucre's ancestors, jeered at religion, sneered at decency. When a plague threatened London one Puritan preacher reasoned, "The cause of the plague is sinne; the cause of sinne is the plays; therefore the cause of the plague is the plays." But Mr. Lucre's cohorts paid no attention to such warnings; they were making money out of their muck. So one morning in 1642 officers of the new Puritan government came walking down the streets of London posting signs upon the theatres. They read: "This theatre is closed by order of the Lords and Commons because it is subversive of public morals."

"There!" cried Shakespeare, abruptly ending his demonstration. "You see what Christianity did to the theatre again? Repressed it, just as it did the Roman theatre. So my plays had to fight not only Mr. Lucre's mercenary crew, but the hostility of the church."

"Hold your horses!" I said. "You are forgetting the first part of your own picture. It was the church that gave the drama its new birth, nourished it, imbued it with dignity and purpose. Can you blame the church entirely if its child grew up to be a prodigal son?"

"What!" he exclaimed. "Would you overlook the fact that

the church mothered the child for five hundred years but never taught it to read and write?"

"What do you mean?"

"In all that time it produced not a single play that has any merit as literature. Nor any dramatists worthy of the name. It never bothered to study the art of drama as Aeschylus and his successors had developed it. It only exploited drama for its own use. Is it any wonder the child ran away?"

"Perhaps not," I conceded, trying to calm him. "But did you not once plead that justice be seasoned with mercy?"

"What's that got to do with it?"

"What you say about the poor artistic quality of the drama the Christian church produced in those centuries is just. But would it not be the part of mercy to recognize that they did make a permanent contribution to their generations?"

"They contributed dullness," he grumbled. "What else?"

"They made the great stories and teachings of the Bible real and vivid to people who could not read Latin—the only language in which it was available to them. They presented in their own way, naïve and simple as it was, the greatest drama that history records: the life and suffering and crucifixion of Christ."

He was silent. I should have left the matter there, but one further fact was crowding for expression.

"And did they not," I added, "prepare the way for you?"

"Just how?" he demanded.

"By making England a nation of actors and of lovers of drama; by lifting the minds of the people to see beyond their limited horizons the whole range of their spiritual history; and by making them sensitive to the struggles of the human soul."

Shakespeare exploded. "Academic folderol!" he exclaimed.

"You would give the church the credit that belongs to the poets and the artists."

"No," I insisted, "I only want to see both sides of this business and to be fair to both."

He jerked his cape from his arm and put it about his shoulders. Then pointing a long finger at me he fired a parting shot: "I might have known better than to try to teach a professor anything. Read my *Hamlet*. He was always trying to see both sides and never able to make up his academic mind to come out for either. See what happened to him! It will happen to you and your lectures. But you can't say you haven't been warned." With that he vanished.

Yes, I had been warned—by Mr. Lucre against having anything to do with a subject that mixed religion and drama, by Aeschylus against popular ignorance of the nature and history of the dramatic art and against confusing religious influence with religious exploitation, and now by Shakespeare against having any sympathy with a religion that had so long a record of repression of the theatre. Despair overwhelmed me. What was the use of going on with the project?

Then, out of the shadows, I heard a voice speaking so quietly I could not be sure it was more than the evening wind in the trees outside my window. But it seemed to be repeating words quoted by a Galilean prophet twenty centuries ago: "He hath anointed me to preach the gospel to the poor; he hath sent me to heal the broken-hearted, to preach deliverance to the captives, and recovery of sight to the blind, to set at liberty them that are bruised . . ."

Hope returned. This man had been sent; he had come. He had lived and suffered and died—but he had risen, and down through the centuries he had been gently working his way into the hearts of men. Each generation had crucified him again, but they could never keep him in his grave. Slowly, but with eternal persistence, he had been transforming human souls. The stage was the mirror of souls. It must have reflected him at work in those souls. That story must be told.

CHAPTER II

The Influence of Christ in Shakespeare's Plays

BEARING in mind the warnings of Aeschylus and Shakespeare, we now take up the examination of representative English and American dramas to see what influence of Christ we may discover in them. Our criteria will be these three, already mentioned in the Introduction: (1) *the principal characters*—in their actions, and especially in their choices in the great crises of their struggles, have they behaved as if their values, their affections, and their loyalties have been influenced by his life and teachings? (2) *The author's spiritual insight*—does he demonstrate an understanding and insight concerning the spiritual life in harmony with those of Christ? (3) *The total effect of the play upon the audience*—is it one that sends the audience away exalted in spirit and with a deepened sense of fellowship with God and man?

Let us begin with Shakespeare. I once heard of a woman who claimed to be quite successful in the use of a Ouija board. She could summon spirits from the other world and they would spell out messages for her. One day her nephew asked her if she could summon Shakespeare. "Certainly," she answered, and in a few moments her sensitive fingers spelled out, "This is him." Let us proceed with a little more caution and less optimism.

We will not, of course, look for any particular theology in

Shakespeare's plays—either orthodox or heterodox. He had no
interest in theology. But he had a profound interest in the
human soul as a battleground of good and evil and of conflicting loyalties. He broke open his characters in their crises and
revealed the conflicting forces in action. Now when a playwright peers into a soul, what he sees there depends upon his
own spiritual insight, his own understanding of the results of
the action of good and evil. What did Shakespeare see in his
principal characters, what can we learn about his own insight and understanding from what he has revealed in his
plays?

Take, for example, the character of Othello. Those who
have seen Paul Robeson's deeply sensitive interpretation of the
role in Margaret Webster's admirable production can never
forget it. It is the picture of a large and generous soul beset
by the fiendishly clever Iago who, for his own selfish ends,
seeks to destroy Othello. He plants in Othello's heart the seed
of jealousy of his innocent and lovely wife Desdemona. By
every device in the devil's brain Iago causes that seed to take
root, grow, and expand until it finally breaks open the soul
of Othello. What do we see in that soul? We see the destruction, the utter havoc, that jealousy can wreak in the life that
harbors it, even in a life as noble as Othello's.

The destruction has not been rapid; it has come by slow but
malignant growth, encouraged by one whom Othello trusted
as a friend. But when it has become full-grown, a dominant
passion, it consumes him. He loses his self-control, his judgment, his dignity. He grows coarse, brutal, accuses Desdemona
of infidelity, and finally murders her.

Dr. George H. Morrison, closing his analysis of this play,
makes this pertinent comment:

Now what are we to make of the moral order of the world where such things happen? There is no happy ending here—no poetic justice—no interference of high heaven to stop these awful happenings. There is no hint, within the limits of the play, that in a future world there is going to be a recompense for wrong. We are left with the wreckage of happiness; the ruin of beautiful and noble lives; the triumph of malignity; the victory of evil. . . .

Where do [the reader's] sympathies lie? Does he crown Iago as a victor? Does he not deeply feel that Iago (apart from any torture that may await him: V, ii, 369) is ruined, lost, and damned, an outcast from the light, unclean, a living death? And with equal intensity does he not feel, even to the point of tears, that it were ten thousand times better to be Desdemona in her gentleness, ten thousand times better to be Othello, for all his sin and suicide, than the vile wretch whose evil slew them?

That is the moral power of Shakespeare. He never twists the facts. But he leaves you, in the midst of hideous facts, loathing the evil, cleaving with all your being to what is high and true and good, spite of its sin and failure, and so aligning yourself, perhaps unconsciously, with the Eternal, who reigns, though clouds and darkness are around His throne.[1]

Let us take another example of Shakespeare's principal characters—Macbeth. Here is a study of a great soul brought to his ruin not by jealousy but by an overweening ambition and the corrosive power of his own success. He is introduced to us as a good and able man. Of himself he says:

> I dare do all that may become a man;
> Who dares do more is none.
>
> (ACT I, SC. 7)

[1] George H. Morrison, *Christ in Shakespeare* (London: James Clarke and Co., 1928), pp. 118–119. Used by permission.

He sincerely wants to serve his country in its hour of need. But he also wants to serve his own interests, to advance his prestige, to get on. And he has never thought through the question: which of these comes first, or which would he sacrifice for the other? He is therefore in a state of unstable equilibrium—a perilous condition for any man, especially one as gifted but as weak-willed as Macbeth.

From the opening scene of the play to its climax Shakespeare puts him under a series of temptations from without and within. The witches, whom he regards as supernatural beings with foreknowledge of things to come, predict a future for him brighter than he had dreamed of. Lady Macbeth, whom he loves and trusts, fans this spark to a flame and belittles the consequences of any small shedding of blood that may be necessary to accomplish his advance toward the throne. "A little water" will wash away the blood stain, she argues. Had Macbeth been clearheaded about his standard of values, had he not been irresolute, he would not have allowed either the witches or his unscrupulous wife to tempt him—but he did. Yet not without some misgivings, for soon we hear him saying:

> Stars, hide your fires,
> Let not light see my black and deep desires.
> (ACT I, SC. 4)

But his misgivings fade when his own success whets his ambition. He is successful in quelling a rebellion of the Western clans of Scotland, and soon thereafter in defeating an attempt at invasion by the King of Norway. He begins a triumphal march to report these victories to Duncan, his king. Along the march the people hail him as the saviour of their country. His head is turned by their plaudits and at this moment the witches meet him again and prophesy yet greater success if he will but claim it. Lady Macbeth points the way—the murder of Duncan. He accomplishes the murder and becomes king himself. But the sons of Duncan—Macduff and Malcolm—escape to England.

Macbeth is now secure upon the throne, but the witches have said that the sons of Banquo, a general, will succeed Macbeth. Will he agree to this and rest content with his present power? His conscience warns him:

> My more-having would be as a sauce
> To make me hunger more.
>
> (ACT IV, SC. 3)

But his ambition says no and ambition wins. So murder follows murder. He orders the execution of General Banquo and his sons, then of Lady Macduff and her sons. His own wife, meanwhile, finds that "a little water" will not wash out the "damned spot" of blood of these crimes; she goes insane and dies. Duncan's son, Macduff, returns from England, heads an avenging army, defeats the forces of Macbeth and slays this ambitious monarch who had become a ruthless and bloody tyrant.

But before Macbeth dies Shakespeare lets us look into his tortured soul. Here is a man who has achieved the highest earthly success—power, wealth, dominion—by following his ambition. But it has been at a cost of honor, justice, and righteousness. He has found no happiness, no security, no peace. His life has been but "a tale told by an idiot, full of sound and fury, signifying nothing." Shakespeare does not preach about it. He shows the whole tragic story in terms of action—action not imposed by some outward fate, but made inevitable by the inner weakness of a man who has allowed his ambition for his own advancement to devour his finer nature. And who does not see the play, or read it, without hearing in his own memory the words of Christ, "What shall it profit a man if he shall gain the whole world, and lose his own soul?"

One more of Shakespeare's studies of individual character— King Lear. In this dramatic poem he portrays a soul, not destroyed by sin as were Othello and Macbeth, but purified through suffering. Again we have a kingly character whose struggle is not peculiar to kingship but common to all humanity. It is the struggle of a man to reintegrate his life after his world has gone to pieces through his own pride and folly.

Shakespeare introduced Othello and Macbeth as likable, even admirable, men. In contrast, he introduces Lear as a thoroughly unlikable, stupid, hot-tempered and arbitrary old despot. In the first scene Lear announces that he is going to shake off the cares of kingship so that he may spend his remaining years unburdened. To that end he has divided his kingdom into three parts—but not equal parts—each to be the dowry of one of his three daughters, Goneril the oldest, Regan the next, and Cordelia the youngest. He declares that the one who protests the greatest love for him will receive the largest share. Thereupon Goneril and Regan vie with each other in flattering protestations of their love. Although they are both married they insist that all their love really belongs to him. He revels in their flattery.

Honest Cordelia will not stoop to dissemble her love. "I cannot heave my heart into my mouth," she says humbly.

> You have begot me, bred me, loved me: I
> Return those duties back as are right fit,
> Obey you, love you, and most honor you.
>
> (ACT I, SC. I)

Beyond that she cannot go, except to add that when she marries she will give half her love to her husband. Enraged, the old king disinherits her, divides her portion between Goneril and Regan, and banishes the faithful Earl of Kent who dared to interpose in Cordelia's behalf. After such an introduction to Lear we are prepared to see him get his "comeuppance" and, whatever it is, he deserves it.

We have not long to wait. The king spends alternately a month at the courts of Goneril and Regan. Now that they have his lands and his regal power they drop their flattery and subservience. They become disrespectful and cruel to him. They deprive him of his attendants and generally so bedevil him that he finally rushes from their castle and goes out upon the open heath in the midst of a severe storm—a storm that matches the tumult in his own breast. Only two accompany him—his court fool and the faithful Kent who had returned in disguise from his banishment in order to serve his king. They take refuge in a hovel. Here Lear, in a frenzied defiance of the storm and of his ungrateful daughters and all who have deserted him, drives himself insane.

This is but the beginning of his descent into purgatory. We shall not follow him through its fiery torments. Penniless, mad, his life sought by his enemies, he wanders about the heath unrecognized and unhonored save by the steadfast Kent. Gloucester seeks to befriend him but Regan's husband frustrates the attempt by tearing out Gloucester's eyes. Cordelia, in France, raises an army to rescue her father and brings a doctor to treat his mind. The doctor succeeds but the army fails, and Cordelia and Lear are taken prisoner. Cordelia is hanged and the old king dies of a broken heart.

But the Lear who dies is a vastly changed man from the one we saw in the first scene. Then he was proud, arrogant, vain, flattery-loving, and concerned with the pomp and circumstance of power. Now, refined by the fires of the purgatory through which he has passed, and redeemed by love, he is humble, gentle, appreciative, self-effacing, and concerned with the simple joys of life. Then he was a king—and miserable. Now he is a prisoner, soon to die, but filled with the joy of one who has learned the true values in life. Hear him speak to Cordelia:

> . . . . Come, let's away to prison:
> We two alone will sing like birds i' the cage;
> When thou dost ask me blessing, I'll kneel down
> And ask of thee forgiveness: so we'll live,
> And pray, and sing, and tell old tales, and laugh
> At gilded butterflies, and hear poor rogues
> Talk of court news; and we'll talk with them too,
> Who loses and who wins, who's in, who's out;
> And take upon's the mystery of things,
> As if we were God's spies: and we'll wear out,
> In a wall'd prison, packs and sects of great ones
> That ebb and flow by the moon. . . .
> Wipe thine eyes;
> The good-years shall devour them, flesh and fell,
> Ere they shall make us weep. . . .
>
> (ACT V, SC. 3)

Yes, a changed man—purified in the furnace of suffering and spiritually reborn through the forgiving love of Cordelia whom he had wronged. That is what Shakespeare saw in the soul of King Lear. But he would not have seen it, or communicated it to us, unless his own mind and heart had somehow been sensitized to discern it.

Time would fail us if we were to tell the stories of the other great tragic characters Shakespeare created in this decade (1599–1609) when his genius, burning its brightest, concentrated its flame upon the destiny of men as determined by their own inner drives. For there is Brutus, a heroic spirit driven by a lofty idealism but failing in common sense, yet rising again superior to his disaster. And Hamlet, the scholar, whose indecision and procrastination and delayed obedience brought ruin on those he loved. And Iago, the incarnation of moral evil, whose love of self made him the destroyer of the love of others. And many more.

Pondering these characters, what insights of Shakespeare are common in his portrayal of all of them? These four at least:

1. There is an inexorable moral order in the universe. The character who defies it will sooner or later be overtaken by retributive justice. As a man soweth, so shall he reap. The wages of sin is death. Not once does Shakespeare allow sentimentality or softness of heart to blind him to this fact and give a happy ending to a character who has persistently ignored or defied the moral order.

2. Man is morally responsible for his own choices and actions. Various characters may blame the gods or their ancestors, or "the slings and arrows of outrageous fortune" for the disasters that befall them. But before the reader completes any of these plays he knows that for Shakespeare the catastrophe of the character is unmistakably due to some inner weakness. This is not to say that a man controls his destiny. Far from it. As Margaret Webster puts it, "there is in all the tragedies [of Shakespeare] the feeling of a terrible force which the weakness or evil in man sets in motion but whose direction he

is powerless to control." [2] The characters in the tragedies have different views about the nature and origin of this "terrible force." Hamlet says:

> There's a divinity that shapes our ends
> Rough-hew them how we may.

Kent declares:

> It is the stars,
> The stars above us, govern our conditions.

Juliet complains:

> . . . that heaven should practice stratagems
> Upon so soft a subject as myself!

Gloucester mourns:

> As flies to wanton boys, are we to the gods.
> They kill us for their sport.

Shakespeare's own views can never be determined from the mouths of his characters. But Miss Webster is surely right when, after long study of the tragedies, she holds that his dramatic credo is best expressed in the lines of Edmund in *King Lear:*

This is the excellent foppery of the world, that when we are sick in fortune—often the surfeit of our own behavior—we make guilty of our disasters the sun, the moon and stars: as if we were villains by necessity, fools by heavenly compulsion; knaves, thieves and treacherers, by spherical predominance; drunkards, liars and

[2] Margaret Webster, *Shakespeare Without Tears* (New York: Whittlesey House, 1942), p. 226. Used by permission.

adulterers, by an enforced obedience of planetary influence; and all that we are evil in, by a divine thrusting-on: an admirable evasion of whoremaster man, to lay his goatish disposition to the charge of a star!

(ACT I, SC. 2)

Whatever the "terrible force" that controls man's destiny, for Shakespeare it is the force that works through the moral law and in the heart of man.

3. Success and failure in life are internal, not external. The rewards and penalties of heaven are not in man's outer circumstance—his purse, his power, his prestige—they are in the wealth or poverty of his soul. In the eyes of the world the king, the potentate, the victorious general are the ones to be applauded and envied. But Shakespeare moves his audiences to applaud those characters who through trial and tribulation maintain or develop an inner integrity, a loyalty to justice, a compassion for the poor, and a humility of mind. This is the inner wealth that thieves cannot break into and steal. It is abiding. King Lear found this inner wealth; Macbeth did not. Lear, marching joyously to prison and death, is far more to be envied than Macbeth at the height of his kingly glory. This appraisal by Shakespeare takes on a prophetic quality when we remember that he wrote *King Lear* and *Macbeth* during the reign of the weak James I when court life was corrupt and civil abuses rife.

4. The human soul has infinite possibilities for good or evil. It is no superficial or romantic glorification of the human race as a whole that he inspires in us, but a belief in the capacity and power of the individual soul. It shines like a morning star through the gloom of Shakespeare's tragedies. We cannot dwell long in the company of even such great sinners as Caesar and

Brutus, Macbeth and Lear, without feeling the vast dimensions of their spiritual natures. We cry with Hamlet:

What a piece of work is man! how noble in reason! how infinite in faculty! . . . in action, how like an angel! in apprehension, how like a god!

(ACT II, SC. 2)

Such are the insights of Shakespeare common to all his major plays and especially his tragedies. They do not constitute a system of theology, but who can contemplate them without recognizing that they are among the basic insights of Christ?

Here let us be cautious and make no extravagant claims, either for Shakespeare or for Christ. It may help to keep us objective if we compare the similarities and the differences between Christ's insights and those of Shakespeare at the focal point of their chief interest—the human soul.

First, the *differences*. Christ looked upon the soul of man with infinite hope. The woman taken in adultery, the hated publican, the thief on the cross—these and many others would witness that he not only understood them but had hope for them no matter how low they had sunk. And when one considers the job lot of humanity he chose for his first disciples he cannot but conclude that Christ must have had a boundless hope if he thought he could make anything out of them.

Shakespeare, on the other hand, seems to be devoid of any such quality as hope or its counterpart, fear, as he looks into a soul. He is entirely objective. He wants to see what is there, no more and no less. And he feels no responsibility whatever for the future of the character. Whether the character gives himself to a devil of lust or greed or ambition, or spurns these and chooses to follow the better angels, is no concern of Shakespeare. What interests him is the discovery and linking of the cause-and-effect sequence of the character's destiny.

Christ's hopefulness was no doubt rooted in his gospel—his good news that God loves the sinner and wants to save him. He demands that the sinner repent, change his direction, and make a fresh start; if he will do that, God's grace will work a transformation in his life. The vilest of sinners can be redeemed by this grace.

Shakespeare has no such gospel. Macbeth, Iago, Regan and Goneril are not saved. In them we find no repentance, and no redeeming grace. They grow harder and harder and at the end of the play seem hell-bound. Lear is the one exception. He suffers, repents, and through the sacrificial love of Cordelia has a spiritual rebirth.

Christ had a concern for humanity in the mass as well as for the individual. He had a compassion for the poor and the disinherited. He held before them a vision of the Kingdom of God, embracing all his children—a Kingdom in which his will would be done on earth as in heaven.

Shakespeare gives but little thought to the masses and none to the Kingdom of God or any kind of Utopia. He sees great social evils and social goods all rooting in some individual's sin or virtue. Thus, the wretched condition of Scotland to him stems from the sins of Macbeth; the times are out of joint and rotten-ripe for change in Denmark because Prince Hamlet's mother was guilty of murder and incest. And it was the pure love of Romeo and Juliet that brought about the reconciliation of the political factions headed by the Montagues and Capulets.

Second, the *similarities*. Christ and Shakespeare both centered their attention primarily on the individual soul. Christ grounded his work and his teaching on man as an individual unit. He chose his disciples one by one. Most of the stories in the gospels show him dealing with men and women—one at a time—with Zacchaeus the publican, with the woman at the well, with the rich young ruler, with Peter and James and John. His parables deal with individuals—with the shepherd who had lost a sheep, the woman who had lost a coin, the father who had a wayward son.

Shakespeare, likewise, concentrates on the individual. He studied and meditated long on the history of his country and the ebb and flow of its political and social movements, but in his dramas he deals with these only as background. He devotes himself much more to the kings than to their kingdoms. Of his chronicle plays, three (*King John, Richard II,* and *Henry VI*) are studies in kingly weakness, and three (*Henry IV, Henry V,* and *Richard III*) are studies in kingly strength. And in all his other plays the abiding impression upon the reader is not of the history, but of the individual characters—Shylock, Antonio, Caesar, Brutus, Mark Antony, Macbeth, Othello, Lear and the rest of the immortal gallery that includes more than two hundred and fifty individual portraits. In all of them he seems continually searching for the secrets of their individuality—their motives, standards of value, whatever it is that makes them tick.

Christ and Shakespeare had similar views of the destructive effects of sin upon the soul. For both, its origin was in some form of selfishness. A man who puts his own welfare or advancement before that of his family, or his community, or his country, or humanity, or God, is violating the moral order of the universe. The inexorable effect of that violation is suffering—suffering that afflicts the sinner and also reaches out and stabs the innocent. Ultimately sin disintegrates and destroys the soul and brings ruin upon the community. The wages of sin is death. Christ preached it, Shakespeare poi-trayed it.

Both Christ and Shakespeare count love the supreme virtue in the human soul and the lack of love the most damning sin. Neither conceives love in the popular terms of boy-meets-girl followed by hot kisses, the marriage bed, and lasting happiness. That conception, common enough on stage and screen, was not in the mind of either Christ or Shakespeare. Love for them meant something less selfish and possessive, more lofty and spiritual. Christ usually spoke of it in terms of the family— the love of a father or mother for their children, or a man for his brother or friend. Shakespeare portrays it in terms of romance, but more than physical; it is the deep affection of the soul for that which has eternal worth in other persons: a com-pound of beauty, truth, and goodness. Its manifestations for him were in understanding, sympathy, sincerity, humility and kindness. Such was the love of Romeo and Juliet. For both Christ and Shakespeare love was the sovereign passion of life, subduing all lower passions, expanding the soul, liberating the oppressed. It demanded one's all even to the sacrifice of one's self upon a cross. And in the end it would draw all men to it, reconciling them to each other and to God.

As for the most damning sin, the wrath of Christ is poured out not on harlots, thieves, publicans, and other ordinary sin-ners, but upon the respectable and intellectual hypocrites, the scribes and pharisees, who had no love in their hearts for the people or for God. Dante, with a kindred understanding, in his *Divine Comedy,* pictures the lowest region of hell as a zone of ice in which were imprisoned the souls of those who on earth had driven all love from their hearts. In like manner

Shakespeare portrays as his supreme villain not one who had committed some crime of passion or dishonesty, but a respectable and intellectual hypocrite—Iago—who had no spark of love for anyone but himself, and who devoted his scheming brain to destroying Othello's love for Desdemona.

One more similarity. In spite of the grief and misery of this world, of man's inhumanity to man and the destruction and waste caused by pride and selfishness, both Christ and Shakespeare have made us see that life can be radiant. No one can read the gospel story without coming to that conviction. It is the very essence of the good news. Nor can one read the plays of Shakespeare without the same conviction. Even in the tragedies a light shines. The evil of the villains calls out the heroism and the sacrifice of others. Thus Iago is finally undone by the assertion of a courage in his wife Emilia which we never suspected was there, and the ugliness in the spirits of Lear and his hypocritical daughters calls out the beauty in the soul of Cordelia to oppose it.

> There is some soul of goodness in things evil
> Would men observingly distil it out.

"Where evil is given its largest freedom and amplest triumph," says Professor Dinsmore, commenting on this aspect in Shakespeare, "it serves to disclose a spiritual grandeur in the soul of man which is superior to the assaults of evil and the wreckage of fortunes [3]. . . . From Brutus to Prospero and Queen Katherine he ceaselessly reiterates the thought that there is something in the soul that does not yield to disaster but is ennobled by it." [4]

[3] Charles Allen Dinsmore, *The Great Poets and the Meaning of Life* (Boston: Houghton Mifflin Co., 1937), p. 210. Used by permission.
[4] *Ibid.*, p. 214.

Obviously the similarities in their insights concerning the soul are more vital than their differences. This fact alone may be the reason why the two books commonly counted most potent in the development of the Christian culture are the Bible and the collected plays of William Shakespeare.

CHAPTER III

From Shakespeare to Shaw

THE choice of Shakespeare for our first brief study was inevitable, but who comes next? Even before his death the decay of the drama, reflecting the decay in the social and political life of the times, had set in. As Nellie Burget Miller sums it up:

> . . . there were signs of the passing of the high idealism which had marked the Renaissance. Puritanism was developing. The nation was to alternate between ascetism and indulgence, and the drama of the Restoration was to make a last pitiful attempt to stand for the joys of sense and the world.[1]

As a matter of fact, during the three hundred years following Shakespeare not much significant or lasting drama was written in England and none in America. A few skilled craftsmen —principally John Dryden and Thomas Otway—made serious attempts to revive blank verse tragedy in the Shakespearean tradition but they lacked his genius, his passion, and most of all his spiritual insight. Popular taste passed to opera and spectacle and then to comedies of intrigue which merged in the early eighteenth century into sentimental comedies. Richard Steele (co-author with Addison of *The Spectator*) is the outstanding figure here. He wrote *The Christian Hero* and a number of plays of a moralistic nature. Sentimentalism gave

[1] Nellie Burget Miller, *The Living Drama*. Century Co., 1924. Used by permission.

place to the anti-sentimental movement under Sheridan and Goldsmith, Goldsmith giving us *She Stoops to Conquer,* and Sheridan *The Rivals* and *The School for Scandal.* Thereafter the drama in England declined almost to the vanishing point.

Why? These reasons stand out among many: the deep interest in religion which had marked the seventeenth century had been followed by an era of skepticism led by the French rationalists. French skeptics dominated not only the politics and the philosophy of Europe but its art as well. Skepticism produced few creative artists. Moreover the theatre had come more and more to be dominated by Mr. Lucre and his commercialists. The drama once again passed through the phases of its origin in worship, its rise to its height as an art that seeks to interpret life, its decline in amusement that seeks only escape from life, and then to a "show business" conducted for revenue only.

It might have remained dead or dormant had not the people of Europe begun to feel the pulse of a new creative movement. Starved by an age of skepticism, they were ready again for men of faith to express the deeper hungers of their hearts. Goethe, Lessing, and Schiller led the new creative movement in Germany; Wordsworth, Coleridge, Shelley, Keats, Carlyle, Tennyson, and Browning in England. It bloomed first in poetry, as it usually does, but poets sooner or later arrive at drama as Shakespeare had done. And soon in Norway came Ibsen, a dramatist who was essentially a poet, with his revolutionary development of the theatre of ideas. With Ibsen the modern drama had its rebirth. Within fifty years it had spread to Russia and throughout the Continent and Britain. These poets were believers, not in orthodox Christianity, but in those basic principles of the faith that Jesus had proclaimed—in the dignity and worth of the individual as a child of God, in the necessity for freedom for his development, and in the Universe as friendly to men of good will.

If our study could be extensive enough to cover even the Western World we should follow Shakespeare with Goethe and Ibsen and Tolstoi. But we have limited ourselves to English and American dramatists, and even among these we must select only a few representative authors. As the first of the moderns in England whose works promise enduring value, let us consider George Bernard Shaw. He is an avowed follower of Ibsen and he claims comparison with Shakespeare. Whether or not Shakespeare would agree with the claim need not concern us here.

Born in Dublin in 1856 of a father who was a corn-dealer and a mother who had a talent for music, his early years were spent in none-too-genteel poverty, for his father drank up the profits of the business and the relatives then ostracized the family. Shaw aptly called himself the "upstart son of a downstart." The influences that seem most marked upon the growing boy were his father (whose bad example probably accounted for George's teetotalism), these self-righteous relatives (who sparked his first fiery criticism of the pretensions of middle-class respectability), and his musical and hardworking mother (who developed in him a deep appreciation of Bach, Handel, Mozart, Beethoven, and Wagner and thus laid the foundation for his later work as music critic for the *Saturday Review*). In school, he declared, he "learned next to nothing," but he read widely, especially in the King James Bible and the works of John Bunyan which, as John Gassner has said, "have made more English writers than all the school-masters of Great Britain and America."

At the age of twenty, fed up with a dreary clerkship in a real estate office, he left Dublin for London where his mother had preceded him. She earned a meagre living as a music teacher while he did literary hackwork and studied. The next few years were filled with the agony of trial and error and failure as he endeavored to get his feet on the first rungs of the ladder of recognition as a creative writer. By the time he had reached twenty-seven he had written four novels, all financial failures. But he kept on growing and his determination sharpened on adversity.

One day in 1882, during a period of hard times for the country as well as for himself, he listened to a lecture by the great single-taxer, Henry George, advocating the "abolition of all taxes for revenue except a tax levied on the value of land irrespective of improvements." The effect upon his thinking was revolutionary. Until then he had dabbled in economics and social philosophy as a natural reaction to his own poverty and frustrations, and he had shown an interest in the current discussions on Darwinism. But Henry George started him on the road to what Shaw called the "economic basis" for a more equitable social order. He began to read socialist literature, and in particular the works of Karl Marx. The more he read the more excited he became and he was soon making friends with other young socialists: Sidney and Beatrice Webb, William Morris, H. G. Wells. Joining these in founding the Fabian Society to promote socialist ideals and philosophy, he went about orating in lecture halls and debating in Hyde Park with all the zeal of an evangelist. He habitually interrupted and heckled speakers who upheld the status quo, and he gained notoriety with some groups and popularity with others by his ability to puncture conventional thinking with his keen wit.

From this time on he had a cause to fight for and he devoted his pen and his voice to it. He would earn his living as he could, as music critic and art critic, and even as a politician —serving as vestryman and borough councilor for St. Pancras district in London from 1897 to 1903—but the main drive of his life was to persuade the public to see the injustice and other evils of capitalistic and imperialistic nationalism and to turn to the better way of socialism. To that end he chose the drama as the medium best suited for stimulating the thought and emotions of his audiences.

His first play to be produced was *Widowers' Houses* in which he presented a realistic picture of the slum problem and its roots in the system of private profit. The production was applauded by the socialists and booed by others and, as he said, it made him "infamous as a playwright." Since then he has written more than sixty dramas, mostly satirical comedies and all presenting the clash of ideas enlivened by Shavian wit. Ridiculed and damned at first, he has risen to the highest rank among the dramatists of the modern world. He makes no apology for using his plays as vehicles for his social and political ideas, for to him these ideas are truth, and art has no higher function than to present truth persuasively.

It would be entirely possible to fill this volume with his dramas, for the influence of Christ upon them is indelible and few if any of the other playwrights excel Shaw in either interest or power. Obviously, however, our study must not concentrate on the works of only one modern author, so let us deal with but two of Shaw's—*Androcles and the Lion* and *St. Joan* [1]— without pausing to debate the claims of his three score other dramatic works. *Androcles and the Lion* exemplifies his work

[1] Quotations from these plays by special permission of Mr. Shaw.

as a propagandist for basic social and religious ideas; *St. Joan* his work as an artist portraying character. In both, of course, the interplay of ideas bulks large; but in the first it is paramount while in the second it takes subordinate place to character. Both illustrate his intense interest in saints and their conflicts with the social order.

Androcles and the Lion, written in 1912 and published three years later, is a dramatic fable in two acts and a prologue. The prologue presents a Shavian adaptation of the old story of a lion with a huge thorn in one of its paws befriended by a man who extracts the thorn. In Shaw's version the man, Androcles, is one of the early Christians—"a small, thin, ridiculous little man of thirty or thirty-five," a gentle soul, henpecked by his overstuffed wife. He fears her but defies her in his compassion for the lion and removes the thorn. The scene ends as the grateful lion dances merrily with Androcles while the wife cries angrily, "Oh, you coward, you haven't danced with me for years!"

The first act takes place some time later at the junction of three roads converging on Rome. It introduces a group of captive Christians being taken to the Colosseum where in the arena the women and weaker men will be thrown to the lions and the stronger men forced to fight the gladiators. It is a motley crowd, the soldiers weary and dusty but dogged, the Christians encouraging one another and making light of their hardships. It appears that along the march the Christians have been showing kindness to the soldiers, repairing their uniforms, cooking their meals, and writing letters for them. This has made the soldiers somewhat dependent upon them to the annoyance of their officers. Now as they approach Rome their Captain orders all such fraternization to cease. In addressing

Christians in the future soldiers must "express abhorrence and contempt. Any shortcoming in this respect will be regarded as a breach of discipline."

Nevertheless when the Captain himself is not on duty he seeks the company of Lavinia, a "good-looking and resolute young woman," and endeavors to persuade her to abandon her faith, offer the pinch of incense to the Roman gods and thus save herself. She can have her choice of four officers and a comfortable home. She prefers martyrdom. Truth, he tells her, needs no martyrs. "Then why kill me?" she asks. Whereupon he reminds her that Christians are not allowed to put questions to which the military regulations provide no answers.

Now come two new Christian captives to join the procession: Ferrovius and Androcles. Ferrovius is a huge man with the strength of an elephant and the temper of a bull. From his youth he has been trained as a warrior and has acquired a wide reputation as such. His conversion to Christianity has put a terrific strain upon his ferocious instincts. He seems a fitting object for ridicule by a young court dandy, Lentulus, who happens to be passing on his road to Rome. He asks Ferrovius if he really turns the other cheek when struck. "Yes, by the grace of God, I do, now," answers Ferrovius. Thereupon Lentulus strikes him. Without flinching Ferrovius turns the other cheek and receives a somewhat feebler blow.

LENTULUS: You know, I should feel ashamed if I let myself be struck like that, and took it lying down. But then I'm not a Christian: I'm a man. (*Ferrovius rises impressively and towers over him. Lentulus becomes white with terror . . .*)

FERROVIUS (*with the calm of a steam hammer*): I have not always been faithful. The first man who struck me as you have struck me was a stronger man than you: he hit me harder than I expected. I was tempted and fell. . . . I never had a happy moment after that until I had knelt and asked his forgiveness by his bedside in the hospital. (*Putting his hands on Lentulus' shoulders with paternal weight*) But now I have learned to resist with a strength that is not my own. I am not ashamed now, nor angry.

LENTULUS (*uneasily*): Er—good evening. (*He tries to move away*).

FERROVIUS (*gripping his shoulders*): Oh, do not harden your heart, young man. Come, try for yourself whether our way is not better than yours. I will now strike you on one cheek; and you will turn the other and learn how much better you will feel than if you give way to the promptings of anger.

Lentulus calls on the Centurion for protection, but in vain. He tries to bribe Ferrovius with no better result. Finally he makes an abject apology. This greatly pleases Ferrovius who, counting such humility the first step toward conversion, begins an effort to make a Christian out of him. He tells Lentulus of a miracle which had attended his efforts in a similar case where another golden-haired youth had struck him and scoffed at him.

FERROVIUS: I sat up all night with that youth wrestling for his soul; and in the morning not only was he a Christian, but his hair was as white as snow. (*Lentulus falls in a dead faint*) There, there: take him away. The spirit has overwrought him.

In conflict with their persecutors the Christians thus give good account of themselves. But when left alone they fall to talking of their inner doubts—not of Christ and his way—but of their ability to meet bravely and humbly the death in the arena toward which they are marching. Doubts, too, about the nature of their life after death. Lavinia isn't sure that she will be acceptable in heaven: she is not constantly Christian but has moments when she forgets all about it. Ferrovius fears he will be tempted to lay out some gladiator. Androcles wants to be reassured that there will be animals in heaven—he loves them so. In the midst of these misgivings an ox-driver arrives demanding that the soldiers clear out of the way and let him pass with his cage carrying a new lion to the Colosseum, for the lion is a part of the Emperor's menagerie service. This angers the Centurion who stands up for his claim to the right of way. "If the lion is menagerie service, the lion's dinner is menagerie service, too. So back with you to your bullocks double quick; and learn your place. March. (*The soldiers start.*) Now then, you Christians: step out there."

The second act brings the great hour of testing as the Christians are herded into the place behind the Emperor's box where the "performers" assemble before entering the arena, which the audience sees through a passageway under the box. At one side of this passageway are the Christians, on the other side the gladiators. The lions are already in their cages in the arena. From the conversation between the manager of the day's program ("the Editor") we learn that the lions are hungry and that the gladiators are picked men and the Emperor's favorites; no one will have a chance against them.

The Emperor (Caesar) arrives eager for the show. The gladiators hail him with the traditional "those about to die salute thee." Lavinia hails him with, "Blessing, Caesar, and forgiveness!" Caesar misinterprets the greeting and replies that there is no forgiveness for Christianity. Lavinia explains that she meant that the Christians forgave him. The whole group of Christians cry Amen. Caesar considers this an impertinence due to their hopelessness. He then turns his attention to Androcles and wants to know if he can perform any miracles today. Androcles answers that he can cure warts by rubbing them with his tailor's chalk, and he can live with his wife without beating her. Caesar promises him speedy relief from her.

Ferrovius is next to receive Imperial notice. Caesar wants this giant as a member of his Pretorian Guard and promises that if he comes out of the arena alive he will make him a member of it with no questions asked about his faith. But Ferrovius insists that he will not fight; he prefers to die. "Better stand with the archangels than with the Pretorian Guard." To which Caesar replies that perhaps the archangels, whoever they are, would perfer to be recruited from the Pretorian Guard.

The time has come for the Christians to enter the arena and fight the gladiators. Ferrovius declines armor but accepts a sword. "I'll die sword in hand," he says, "to show people that I could fight if it were my Master's will, and that I could kill the man who kills me if I chose." The trumpet sounds for the entrance. Ferrovius starts convulsively and prays aloud, "Heaven give me strength!" This is attributed to fright, but Ferrovius pauses long enough to explain his inner conflict. When he hears the trumpet, or any other challenge to battle, fire runs through his veins, he must charge, strike, conquer— that has been his whole training. He begs his fellow Christians to exhort him and remind him that if he raises his sword his honor will fall and his Master be crucified afresh. Lavinia tells him that nothing but faith will save him.

FERROVIUS: Which faith? There are two faiths. There is our faith. And there is the warrior's faith, the faith in fighting, the faith that sees God in the sword. How if that faith should overwhelm me?

LAVINIA: You will find your real faith in the hour of trial.

FERROVIUS: That is what I fear. I know I am a fighter. How can I feel sure that I am a Christian?

With this turmoil surging in his breast he turns to his fellow Christians.

FERROVIUS: Brothers: the great moment has come. That passage is your hill to Calvary. Mount it bravely, but meekly; and remember! not a word of reproach, not a blow nor a struggle. Go.

And he leads them into the arena. For the next few minutes there is no sound from that battleground, and we are treated to a sombre love scene in which the Captain begs Lavinia to give up her belief in the Christian fairy stories and marry him. She need only burn the incense even now to free herself.

LAVINA: Handsome Captain: would you marry me if I hauled down the flag in the day of battle and burnt the incense? Sons take after their mothers, you know. Do you want your son to be a coward?

THE CAPTAIN (*strongly moved*): By great Diana, I think I would strangle you if you gave in now.

At this point the Emperor throws open the door of his box and angrily announces to the Editor, the Call Boy, and the remaining gladiators that the Christians will not fight and the gladiators in the ring cannot get their blood up to attack them. It's all the fault of Ferrovius whose blazing eyes control the

situation. Therefore Caesar orders whips and hot irons to pro-
voke the Christians to fight. The whips and irons are brought.
A great clamor bursts out, followed by loud applause. To the
Christians remaining outside it can mean only that their fellows
within are being killed.

But a few moments later the truth comes out: Ferrovius has
killed six gladiators! In his hour of trial, faith in the sword
had overwhelmed him. Caesar rushes from his box to con-
gratulate him and promise him a laurel crown of gold. When
before has one naked man slain six armed men of the
bravest and best? At the climax of his enthusiasm he decrees:
"The persecution shall cease: If Christians can fight like this, I
shall have none but Christians to fight for me. (*To the gladiators*) You are ordered to become Christians, you there: do
you hear?" As for the Christians who were to be thrown to the
lions, let them all be freed; Caesar had never thought of harm-
ing any of them.

The menagerie keeper reminds him, however, that there
must be at least one Christian to feed the new lion; the people
have been promised such a treat and will tear the decorations
down if they are disappointed. Caesar grants this reasonable
request and the lot falls to Androcles. We see him march,
desperately frightened but piteously heroic, into the arena
where he falls on his knees in prayer before the lion's cage. A
gong sounds, the grating of the cage is raised, the lion rushes
out. Androcles crouches and hides his face in his hands. The
lion gathers himself for the spring—then suddenly recognizes
Androcles as the man who had removed the thorn from its
paw. The whole mood of the scene instantly changes to one of
joyous reunion of old friends. Androcles and the lion embrace
rapturously and waltz around the arena amid the deafening

applause of the populace. Caesar in amazement rushes down from his box declaring that he has seen a miracle that convinces him of the truth of Christianity. He has scarcely uttered the words when Androcles and the lion return through the passage and the lion begins a chase of the Emperor that doesn't end until Caesar takes refuge in the arms of Androcles.

Mr. Shaw could hardly have wondered that this comedy, which verges here and there on farce, flabbergasted many of the most respectable people in his audience. He has always delighted in flabbergasting them. But he had a much deeper purpose and fortunately he published it for the benefit of those who must have the meaning of an art-work diagramed. In this play, he said,

I have presented one of the Roman persecutions of the early Christians, not as the conflict of a false theology with a true, but as what all such persecutions essentially are: an attempt to suppress a propaganda that seemed to threaten the interests involved in the established law and order, organized and maintained in the name of religion and justice by politicians who are pure opportunist Have-and-Holders. People who are shewn by their inner light the possibility of a better world based on the demand of the spirit for a nobler and more abundant life, not for themselves at the expense of others, but for everybody, are naturally dreaded and therefore hated by the Have-and-Holders, who keep always in reserve the two sure weapons against them. The first is persecution. . . . The second is by leading the herd to war, which immediately and infallibly makes them forget everything, even their most cherished and hard won public liberties, in the irresistible surge of their pugnacity and the tense preoccupation of their terror. . . .

My martyrs are the martyrs of all time, and my persecutors the persecutors of all time. My Emperor, who has no sense of the value of common people's lives . . . is the sort of monster you can make of any silly-clever gentleman by idolizing him. . . . All my Christians have different enthusiasms, which they accept as the same religion only because it involves them in a common opposition to the official religion and consequently in a common doom. Androcles is a humanitarian naturalist, whose views surprise everybody. Lavinia, a clever and fearless freethinker, shocks the Pauline Ferrovius, who is comparatively stupid and conscience ridden. . . .

But the most striking aspect of the play at this moment [1915] is the terrible topicality given it by the war. We were at peace when I pointed out, by the mouth of Ferrovius, the path of an honest man who finds out, when the trumpet sounds, that he cannot follow Jesus. . . . Great numbers of our clergy have found themselves in the position of Ferrovius. They have discovered that they hate not only their enemies but everyone who does not share their hatred, and that they want to fight and to force other people to fight. . . . It has never occurred to them to take off their black coats and say simply, "I find in the hour of trial that the Sermon on the Mount is tosh, and that I am not a Christian. I apologize for all the unpatriotic nonsense I have been preaching all these years. Have the goodness to give me a revolver and a commission in a regiment which has for its chaplain a priest of the god Mars: *my* God." Not a bit of it. They have stuck to their livings and served Mars in the name of Christ, to the scandal of all religious mankind. . . .

Whether or not the reader agrees with Shaw in his interpretation of war, he will hardly question that this play shows the influence of Christ and of the Sermon on the Mount upon the author, his characters, and his spiritual insights. The total effect of the play upon the audience may be another matter. Many it exalted; others it only angered. That was probably the effect produced by the Sermon on the Mount when it was first uttered.

*   *   *   *   *

An interviewer once asked Shaw why he did not join the Roman Catholic Church. He replied that he felt certain the church would never tolerate two popes. The question would never have been asked if the interviewer had read *St. Joan.*

In his preface to the play—a preface more than half as long as the play itself—he condenses the chronology of Joan into one sentence. "Joan of Arc, a village girl from the Vosges, was born about 1412; burnt for heresy, witchcraft, and sorcery in 1431; rehabilitated after a fashion in 1456; designated Venerable in 1904; declared Blessed in 1908; and finally canonized in 1920." He then characterizes her as "the most notable Warrior Saint in the Christian calendar, and the queerest fish among the eccentric worthies of the Middle Ages . . . a pious Catholic . . . one of the first Protestant martyrs . . . one of the first apostles of Nationalism . . . and the pioneer of rational dressing for women." The play dramatizes the last three years of her brief life—her seventeenth to nineteenth years.

We see her first, an illiterate peasant girl, in a sharp but exhilarating clash with Captain Robert de Baudricourt, a military squire of choleric temper, as she demands of him a horse, a soldier's armor and a few men at arms. She tells him that she has heard the voices of St. Catherine, St. Margaret, and St. Michael; that God through them has commanded her to raise the siege of Orleans and to crown the Dauphin in Reims Cathedral. Therefore she has come to Robert for help. It is as simple as that. The captain is understandably flabbergasted. She has him gasping when she adds that she is also commissioned to drive the English out of France. (She speaks of the English as the "goddams" because that is the word most often on their tongues.) The captain tries to impress her with the outrageousness of all this—does she expect to succeed where the French army has failed? Does she know the strength and terror of the English? In pert reply she says, "You must not be afraid, Robert——" which well-nigh sends him into a fit of apoplexy. But she goes on to assure him that she will teach the French soldiers to fight not to save their own skins as they have been doing so poorly, but to fight that the will of God may be done in France. In the end her sublime audacity wins. She gets the horse, the armor, and the soldiers.

As the play advances we see her at various stages of her swift, victorious march. She puts new life into the French army by her simple faith in God and her daring military strategy—a combination that works miracles. As her victories mount, the whole country swings into line behind her—the generals, the royal court, the church, and the people. She raises the siege of Orleans and crowns the imbecilic Dauphin in Reims Cathedral. Then she wants to go and liberate Paris and drive the English back over the Channel.

But at this point the solid front that has supported her cracks. The generals, the king, and the church unite against her. The proposal is too audacious, the English in the north are too strong, and in spite of what Joan has done thus far God—they tell her—is really on the side of the big battalions. At first they try to dissuade her by reason, but she prefers to follow her "voices." So they apply the compulsions of their royal and ecclesiastical authority. The English feudal lords meanwhile have put a price of sixteen thousand pounds upon her head. The Earl of Warwick makes a compact with Bishop

Cauchon of France to stop the girl. Warwick is opposed to her because she menaces the whole feudal system by her insistence that the king of a country should be the sovereign of the lords and not their servant. Cauchon is opposed to her because she refuses to recognize the authority of the church as superior to the authority of her voices and visions. Warwick wants to be rid of her as a Nationalist. Cauchon wants to be rid of her as a Protestant, although neither term has yet come into use. But Joan defies all argument, all compulsion, all fear, and pushes on with her loyal troops. In her next campaign she is wounded, betrayed, captured, and turned over to the English for the reward.

Now comes the great trial scene. It is an ecclesiastical trial, not a court trial. It takes places in the castle of Rouen where Joan is surrounded by doctors of law and theology and Dominican monks. In dramatic intensity it compares with the trial of Orestes in Aeschylus' *Eumenides* and the trial of Antonio before Portia in *The Merchant of Venice*. With marvelous skill Shaw brings to a climax the pressures of the opposition upon Joan in order to break her open and reveal the innermost struggles of her soul. That opposition charges Joan with being a heretic and a witch, although the issues are occasionally clouded by a square-headed English chaplain who interjects charges that she is a horse thief and that she wears men's clothes.

For eleven weeks the trial has been in progress. Joan has been examined fifteen times by the Bishop's court, but now the Holy Inquisition has been called in and their combined forces, egged on by the Earl of Warwick, concentrate on proving that this nineteen-year-old girl is such a danger to society that she must either recant or be burned. Yet Shaw presents the trial as a fair one—at least as fair as any such trial in the Middle Ages could be. The Bishop, the Prosecutor, and the Inquisitor sincerely want to save the girl's soul. Unless she recants her soul is lost, because she has denied that the authority of the church is superior to the authority of her "voices" which the church insists have been voices of the devil. The Inquisitor would go to the extreme limit of mercy to protect Joan from what he regards as her folly, but heresy is a cancer and if tolerated will spread its malignancy through the church. Therefore the judges, while making every effort to be merciful, must remember that justice demands that heresy must be uprooted.

To these charges Joan gives simple answers. She insists that she is a dutiful child of the church and has never denied its authority, but that she is also a child of God and that the voices that she hears are his commands and must be obeyed. The issue then boils down to this: is she or the church to be the judge as to whether or not the voices are from God?

Joan replies, "What other judgment can I judge by but my own?"

Whereupon Bishop Cauchon demands, "Dare you pretend, after what you have said, that you are in a state of grace?" Joan answers, "If I am not, may God bring me to it; if I am, may God keep me in it!"

"Were you in a state of grace when you stole the Bishop's horse?" cries one of the assessors.

"Oh, devil take the Bishop's horse and you too!" exclaims Cauchon angrily. "We are here to try a case of heresy; and no sooner do we come to the root of the matter than we are thrown back by idiots who understand nothing but horses."

And so the trial proceeds. Finally when Joan is worn to the point of exhaustion and has been assured that she has proven herself guilty of heresy many times, the Executioner is brought in and she is told that he is ready to burn her; that eight hundred English soldiers are waiting to take her to the stake; and that they have built it high so the death will be unusually cruel. It is the breaking point for Joan. She cannot face the pain. Her heart is open before us and we see the devils of fear and doubt struggling against her faith. Her voices had promised her that she would not be burnt, but now the fire is about to be kindled. The voices must have deceived her, betrayed her. She admits it, agrees to sign the recantation, and makes her mark amid the joyous shouts of those who have sought to save her and the angry protests of those who were intent on burning her.

But the trial is not over. The Inquisitor informs her that, while she has escaped the stake, she must do penance for her sin and is therefore condemned to spend the rest of her days in perpetual imprisonment. Her courage returns. "Am I not then to be set free?" she demands. "Give me that writing!" Snatching it, she tears it into fragments. "Light your fire! Do you think I dread it as much as the life of a rat in a hole? My voices were right." And she is led to the stake and burned.

Shaw adds an Epilogue, the scene laid in the bedroom of King Charles the Seventh, twenty-five years later. The principal characters, now all dead, come back as spirits to discuss the deeds of Joan and her trial. They are duly repentant and agree that she was right and they wrong. They look forward to the time when she will be recognized as a saint. This amuses Joan, who has developed a highly Shavian wit. But before the scene ends a gentleman of the year 1920 makes his way into the room and announces that the canonization has been accomplished. Everyone congratulates Joan who then poses this question, "Shall I rise from the dead, and come back to you a living woman?" With one accord they urge her not to do so. The world is not yet ready to receive a living saint. The hour of midnight strikes; the spirits return to the other world; and Joan prays wistfully, "O God that madest this beautiful earth, when will it be ready to receive thy saints? How long, O Lord, how long?"

Such is the action of the play. Essentially it is historically as accurate as any play can be expected to be in the attempt to condense three years of happenings in real life into three hours upon the stage. It is true tragedy, yet it cannot be compared with any of the tragedies of Shakespeare. Shakespeare created his characters, even though men and women of their names existed in history or in earlier plays; Shaw makes no attempt to create Joan. Rather, he brings his expert dramatic craftsmanship to the task of making the historical Joan relive her life before our eyes. Resurrecting a character may be more difficult than creating one. Certainly fewer playwrights have attempted it.

But our study is not concerned with comparison. It is to discover what influence of Christ may be found in this drama. Suppose we apply the three criteria suggested earlier:

1. The central character—at the crisis of her struggle when the author reveals her innermost soul to us is it a soul that shows the impact of Christ? When she makes her great choice that will resolve her conflict and determine her action is it a choice that reflects him? Joan's crisis is when she must choose between denying her faith or being burned at the stake for it. She chooses to die as a Christian martyr.

2. The author's insight concerning the spiritual life as he demonstrates it in the play as a whole—is it in harmony with

the insight of Christ? Shaw epitomizes his insight in a question he puts in the mouth of Cauchon in the Epilogue: "Must then a Christ perish in torment in every generation to save those who have no imagination?" It sounds like the echo of Christ's words, "He who would come after me must take up his cross and follow me."

3. The total effect of the play upon the audience—is it one that sends the audience away exalted in spirit, with a deeper sense of fellowship with God and man? Only those who have seen the play well presented, or have read it for themselves will be able to apply that test. Many have done so and borne witness to the play's power to produce this effect. In fact, Shaw might well be justified if he were to say, with his customary forthrightness, that any person who does not experience a profound catharsis of emotions and a sense of spiritual elevation after living through these tragic hours with St. Joan is a hard-hearted reprobate and will come to no good end.

CHAPTER IV

Other Modern British Drama

HAD this chapter been written thirty-five years ago it would probably have dealt at some length with two plays widely popular at that time in English and American theatres: Charles Rann Kennedy's *The Servant in the House* (1908) and Jerome K. Jerome's *The Passing of the Third Floor Back* (1910). The central character in each play is a human representation of Christ in modern dress, or at least strongly suggests him.

Mr. Kennedy pictures an English family in which two brothers have long been estranged by the intolerances of their differing social castes and political opinions and by deeper conflicts rooted in opposing systems of value. The action takes place in the home of the elder brother, a clergyman in a fashionable parish. In this home the other brother, a cleaner of cesspools, is seldom seen and never welcome. The clergyman expects a visit from a famous church dignitary, the Bishop of Benares, noted for his revolutionary methods in winning converts in India. The bishop comes, but disguised as a servant. Quietly and humbly, in the spirit of Christ, he eventually brings about a reconciliation of the brothers before they recognize him either as the bishop or as their own long-lost brother.

Mr. Jerome in the *The Passing of the Third Floor Back* tells a similar story of a Stranger who comes into an English board-

61

ing house where a motley assortment of self-centered sinners are backbiting and cheating each other. The landlady rents to the Stranger a tiny room—the third floor back—at an exorbitant price which he pays so chivalrously that she promptly reduces it to a more reasonable figure. Then he goes to work upon the boarders one by one, gently bringing out the nobler qualities of each, until by the end of the last act, three weeks later, he has transformed the lot—and vanished.

Sincere and moving as these plays were in their day, they are now seldom mentioned even in the more extensive surveys of drama. They are almost never revived, except by church drama groups. Why? The reason seems to be that they have not stood up under critical examination either as good plays or as realistic religion. They are dramatized sermons in which the characters are moved about as pawns to win the game for the authors' thesis that Christ in human form in our midst would quickly resolve our conflicts and bring a happy ending to our troubles. In neither play is there any recognition of suffering as a part of Christ's role. He wins quickly by sweetness and light. We have come to recognize that there are many Christlike souls in history and among us today, but they have not had such quick and overwhelming success. They have had to carry heavy crosses, and have frequently been hung upon them. The leaven they have planted in human hearts has worked—but slowly. And there is not yet any convincing evidence that if Christ himself were to come among us we would not crucify him again—as indeed we do in our wars and in other denials of our brotherhood.

In our present study we shall steer clear of such plays and trust that the dramas we select will bear up under the critical appraisal of future generations. Among the many English dramatists whose plays deserve consideration here the names of such outstanding writers as John Galsworthy, J. M. Barrie, Stephen Phillips, Somerset Maugham, St. John Ervine, John Masefield, T. S. Eliot, Laurence Housman, Paul Vincent Carroll, Jan Struther, and Emlyn Williams come readily to mind. (For lists of their more important plays see the Appendix.) Each has a definite claim upon our attention, but if we are to stick to our plan of treating a few plays intensively rather that many sketchily we must make a limited selection. After much inner debate I have chosen Galsworthy, Masefield, and Williams because, in addition to being able playwrights, they have such different philosophical approaches to the human struggles they portray. Galsworthy is essentially a stoic, Masefield a Christian mystic, and Williams, the youngest, may be classed for the present as a romantic humanist.

John Galsworthy

Born in 1867, reared in a home of well-to-do and cultured parents, John Galsworthy was educated for the law at Oxford. He practiced but little, preferring to travel and study, and eventually to write. He is one of the few authors who have achieved distinction in both novel writing and drama writing. His *Forsyte Saga* made him famous as a novelist, his *Silver Box, Strife, Justice, The Pigeon, The Skin Game,* and *Loyalties* as a dramatist. In plays as well as novels he reveals a deep passion for social justice—or, more accurately, a deep awareness of the social injustice rife in modern England. Yet his treatment of this theme is never polemic. He is content to paint the picture of it so vividly that his readers and audience will want to seek their own solution. "I look upon the stage," he said, "as the great beacon light of civilization, but the drama should lead the social thought of the time and not direct or dictate it."

If he were alive today and by some strange chance a participant in this discussion he might protest that he never attempted to apply specifically the religion of Christ to the solution of any of the problems of social injustice he has dramatized. This is quite true. To make his position even more emphatic he might go on to say, as he did in his essay entitled "Some Platitudes Concerning the Drama":

A drama must be shaped so as to have a spire of meaning. Every grouping of life and character has its inherent moral; and the business of the dramatist is so to pose the group as to bring that moral poignantly to the light of day. Such is the moral that exhales from plays like *Lear, Hamlet,* and *Macbeth.* But such is not the moral to be found in the great bulk of contemporary drama. The moral of the average play is now, and probably always has been, the triumph at all costs of a supposed immediate ethical good over a supposed immediate ethical evil. . . . It was once said of Shakespeare that he had never done any good to anyone, and never would. This, unfortunately, could not, in the sense in which the word "good" was then meant, be said of most modern dramatists. . . . In truth the good that Shakespeare did to humanity was of a remote, and, shall we say, eternal nature; something of the good that men get from having the sky and the sea to look at.[1]

We would reassure Mr. Galsworthy with a hearty Amen to all that. Further, we believe that one reason why some of his plays seem destined to survive many of his contemporaries' is because he has faithfully followed the principle he has so force-

[1] From *The Inn of Tranquility.* Charles Scribner's Sons, 1931. Used by permission.

fully stated. We shall not, therefore, scan his plays for any moral, in the customary use of that term. In fact, we are not looking for "morals" in this sense in any plays. We are looking only for a sincere interpretation of life by those who see it steadily and see it whole. If, in such interpretations, we find those spiritual insights which were also in Christ, we may point them out. But we shall not try to discover them where they do not exist.

With this as our point of view, let us take up the consideration of Galsworthy's play, *Strife*, in which he dramatizes a struggle between capital and labor. Produced in 1909, it is the first play dealing with a strike situation in modern British drama. He treats capitalists and employees with fairness and objectivity. He is not on either side, but on the side of humanity as a whole.

As the play begins, the strike has already been going on for several months. Both sides have suffered heavy losses—the capitalists in dividends, the miners in savings and even in bread and butter. The capitalists in this struggle are headed by old John Anthony, who has been Chairman of the Board of this Tin Mining Company for thirty years. He has weathered other storms with his workers in years past and has always won out. He believes firmly that the workers should be governed justly but with an iron hand. He thinks they are too ignorant to have any part in determining the labor policies of the Company. The striking miners are headed by David Roberts, a stalwart Scot who seems the very prototype of John L. Lewis. Roberts believes that justice for the workers can be obtained only by breaking the power of capital and by establishing democracy for industry.

Roberts in the play represents the irresistible force, John

Anthony the immovable object. Neither will compromise nor permit his colleagues to compromise. As the play proceeds, terrific pressure is brought upon both men, not only by their followers, but by the members of their families. Old Anthony's son, while loyal to his father, yet has the younger generation's appreciation of the miners' side of the battle. Anthony's daughter is extremely sympathetic with the starving condition of the miners' wives and children. Thus Anthony's son and daughter oppose his unyielding attitude and do all in their power to persuade him to a more humane course.

Likewise, Roberts is put under the pressure of his wife's serious illness resulting from malnutrition and lack of doctor's care. Nevertheless, he is consecreated, heart and soul, to the cause of the strikers and he leaves her bedside to address their meeting. They were on the point of forsaking his leadership and accepting a compromise which their national union had proposed. Listen to Roberts as he takes command:

You've forgotten what that fight 'as been; many times I have told you; I will tell you now this once again. The fight o' the country's body and blood against a blood-sucker. The fight of those that spend themselves with every blow they strike and every breath they draw, against a thing that fattens on them, and grows and grows by the law of *merciful* Nature. That thing is Capital! A thing that buys the sweat o' men's brows, and the tortures o' their brains, at its own price. *Don't* I know that? Wasn't the work o' *my* brains bought for seven hundred pounds, and hasn't one hundred thousand pounds been gained them by that seven hundred without the stirring of a finger? It is a thing that will take as much and give you as little as it can. That's *Capital!* A thing that will say—"I'm very sorry for you, poor fellows—you have a cruel time of it, I know," but will not give one sixpence of its dividends to help you have a better time. That's Capital! Tell me, for all their talk, is there one of them that will consent to another penny on the Income Tax to help the poor? That's Capital! A white-faced, stony-hearted monster! Ye have got it on its knees; are ye to give up at the last minute to save your miserable bodies pain? [2]

By this appeal, he rallies the men to go on with the strike under his leadership. He has barely succeeded when word is brought to him that his wife is dying.

A few minutes later the word that Roberts' wife is dead reaches the executive committee of the Board at its meeting in old Anthony's home. The other members are conscience-stricken. They are ready to go a long way to meet the strikers' demands and prevent further suffering and starvation of women and children. But old Anthony will have none of such "weakness." He insists that if his adversary suffer in fair fight not sought by him it is only the adversary's fault. Hear him as he challenges his colleagues to stand firm:

The men have been treated justly, they have had fair wages, we have always been ready to listen to complaints. It has been said that times have changed; if they have, I have not changed with them. Neither will I. It has been said that masters and men are equal! Cant! There can only be one master in a house! Where two men meet the better man will rule. It has been said that Capital and Labour have the same interests. Cant! Their interests are as wide asunder as the poles. It has been said that the Board is only part of a machine. Cant! We *are* the machine, its brains and sinews; it is for us to lead and to determine what is to be done, and to do it without fear or favour. Fear of the men!

[2] John Galsworthy, *Representative Plays*, pp. 129–30. Charles Scribner's Sons, 1909–1924. Used by permission.

Fear of the shareholders! Fear of our own shadows! Before I am like that, I hope to die. There is only one way of treating "men" —with *the iron hand*. This half and half business, the half and half manners of this generation, has brought all this upon us. Sentiment and softness, and what this young man, no doubt, would call his social policy. You can't eat cake and have it! This middle-class sentiment, or socialism, or whatever it may be, is rotten. Masters are masters, men are men! Yield one demand, and they will make it six. They are (*he smiles grimly*) like Oliver Twist, asking for more. If I were in *their* place I should be the same. But I am not in their place. Mark my words: one fine morning, when you have given way here, and given way there— you will find you have parted with the ground beneath your feet, and are deep in the bog of bankruptcy; and with you, floundering in that bog, will be the very men you have given way to. I have been accused of being a domineering tyrant, thinking only of my pride—I am thinking of the future of this country, threatened with the black waters of confusion, threatened with mob government, threatened with what I cannot see. If by any conduct of mine I help to bring this on us, I shall be ashamed to look my fellows in the face.[3]

Ultimately, after the agony of blood and tears, starvation and death, resulting from these stubborn die-hard tactics, the directors force Anthony to resign and the miners desert the leadership of the unbending Roberts. Both the men of iron are broken. Directors and miners then sign the very compromise settlement that they had rejected at the beginning of the trouble.

Galsworthy tacks on no moral, but any audience that does not see the implications of this play for the extremists in their own strifes is blind indeed.

[3] *Ibid.,* pp. 151–152.

In his comedy entitled *The Pigeon*, produced in 1912, he deals with another social problem: how to treat the down-and-outers. He portrays three human derelicts who, looking for a place to sleep and a bite to eat on a stormy Christmas eve, come to the studio of an artist. This artist is a tender-hearted man who can never turn a deaf ear to a beggar. The first of the derelicts is a flower girl with convenient morals who, when the flower business is poor, earns her living in a furnished room. The second is a young vagabond with an aversion for work who calls himself a philosopher. The third is a rum-soaked old cabman. Before Christmas evening is over, these three have plucked their pigeon—the artist—of his last coins, his food and drink, and even his only pair of trousers.

In the weeks that follow, the artist seeks the help of three friends in dealing with these self-invited guests. One friend is a vicar who tries to reform their morals without touching their springs of action. Another is a professor who has a theory that the government should provide work for such people but doesn't know what to do with them in the meantime. The third is a Justice of the Peace who would turn the deserving poor over to charitable institutions and the undeserving to the devil. All these friends have a go at the beggars—and all fail. By the third act, the derelicts have been sent to institutions of one kind or another where it is hoped they will make as little trouble as possible and eventually die. But they all escape and one at a time, by the end of the play, are back on the hands of the tender-hearted artist.

At first thought, this may seem just a problem play—a satirical study of the futility of various ways of dealing with the poor. It is that—but it is more. Underneath the comedy of the various situations, the play is imbued with a sense of social compassion for the poor. Moreover, we—the audience—come to have an affectionate interest in these down-and-outers, recognizing them as persons very like others we meet every day. Again, the various ways of meeting our responsibility to them is subjected to honest criticism devoid of sentimentality.

What is the outcome of this critical portrayal in the guise of comedy? What is the effect upon us as the audience? We see the pitiful inadequacy of our own efforts to help the poor, whether those efforts be the moralistic kind the vicar uses, or the charitable institution kind of the Justice of the Peace, or the governmental kind of the professor. Only the artist's efforts, bungling as they are, seem to possess the germ of hope. He does not solve the problem of poverty, but he shares his substance with the poor. He does not succeed in getting them on their feet, but he extends to each the sympathy of his understanding heart. That artist, sentimental and foolish as the world counts him, reminds us strongly of one of those surprised persons in Jesus' parable of the final judgment who ask, "Lord, when saw we thee hungry and fed thee, naked and clothed thee, sick and in prison and visited thee?"

Nowhere does Galsworthy say this himself; nowhere does he preach; his task as a dramatist is to present his characters and his story through action and to "soak his play with an inevitability" that convinces his audience. It is the audience that draws the conclusion, not the author.

Loyalties, as the title indicates, deals with the conflict of loyalties which brings tragedy to human life. He shows a group, each member of which has a paramount loyalty. For one it is his race, for another the army, for another his social set, for another her husband, and for another his professional integrity. All are good loyalties. But they bring the characters into increasing conflict and ultimately to the death of one and

misery for others. And the audience, without a line of sermonizing, carries away the inevitable conclusion that its loyalties,
virtuous as they may be, must be subordinated to some over-all
loyalty if they are not to run wild and collide with each other.[4]

In these and all of his plays, Galsworthy departs radically
from the Greek and the Elizabethan models of tragedy. They
centered their dramas around great characters—kings, queens,
tyrants, generals—Galsworthy centers his around ordinary
human beings like ourselves. The Greeks and Shakespeare
broke open individual great souls; Galsworthy breaks open
social problems. They saw one tyrant as the cause of the
people's distress and the waste of human life; Galsworthy sees
modern civilization, with its complex struggles for power, as
that cause. This departure from the classical tradition, which
concentrated on the individual, and the substitution of social
problems of modern civilization as the focus of the dramatist's
thought has demanded a penalty from Mr. Galsworthy: his
plays will probably pass out of currency when these particular
social problems have been replaced by others. Aeschylus and
Shakespeare will still be read when Galsworthy is forgotten. But
this is the penalty any artist pays for adapting his art to the
specific needs of his times. Moreover, the problems with which
Mr. Galsworthy concerns himself are so inherent in the nature
of our social and industrial civilization that they will be with
us for a least a generation or two.

While he has departed from the classical tradition in this
fundamental respect, he has held to it in all others. Character
is still the ultimate determiner of destiny although he sees
character as molded not by individual passion but by social

[4] A more extended review and analysis of *Loyalties* may be found in
my chapter on "The Dramatist and the Minister" in *The Arts and
Religion,* edited by Albert E. Bailey. Macmillan, 1944. F.E.

forces and ideologies. His plots grow out of his characters. The solutions of his plots have the Greek sternness in adherence to the inevitability of cause and effect. He avoids sentimentality as he would a plague. A happy ending is never tacked on to please the audience. His integrity is beyond challenge.

"What he has done," said George Pierce Baker in his introduction to the volume *Representative Plays by John Galsworthy*, "names him the master realist of English drama today. . . . What he has written . . . is dramatized social history." [5] Yes, Galsworthy had the qualities he admired in other great dramatists—"a deep indignant pity, piercing vision, and a sensitiveness seldom equalled . . ." They are also the qualities of a religious prophet.

John Masefield

John Masefield represents an aspect of life and letters in modern England quite different from Shaw and Galsworthy. He is frankly a mystic and a Christian. Born at Ledbury in 1875, he ran away from home at the age of fourteen and went to sea. After many months of adventures and misadventures as a sailor he landed in New York with only "a whole suit of clothes, a sound pair of shoes, and an unquenchable spirit." He found odd jobs on farms and in factories and for a time served as bartender. He was often without food and shelter. When he eventually returned to London he began to write. He made friends with two Irish playwrights, Yeats and Synge, and under their influence turned his developing talents to drama and poetry.

He has written nearly a score of plays and several volumes

[5] *Ibid.*, p. xxi.

of essays and poems. Among the latter, "Salt Water Ballads," "The Widow in the Bye Street," "Dauber," and "The Story of a Round-House," are probably best known. His freshness of spirit, salty as sea air, his lively imagination, his disciplined allegiance to the classical poetical forms so nobly upheld by Tennyson, his deep interest in mysticism, and his honest concern for the lot of the common man combine to give his poetry a quality that won for him the honorary office of Poet Laureate at the age of fifty-five.

Professor Allardyce Nicholl, characterizing his creative genius as a dramatist, writes, "He is by spirit sternly classical; endowed with passion . . . full of the fantasy of the poetic genius . . . a confirmed realist; clinging tensely to the natural world, he is wrapped in the spirit of mysticism." Such a mixture of conflicting traits might well produce a lunatic or at least a split personality. But Masefield has a strong integrating force working within him—his religion.

Usually, in essays dealing with his dramas, his most noted play, *The Tragedy of Nan*, written in 1908, is chosen for specific examination, but for our present purpose let us select another, written twenty years later—*The Coming of Christ*. It was not written for the theatre, but for a special Whitsuntide service at Canterbury Cathedral. Imagine, then, instead of a theatre stage the stately nave of the great cathedral with its eighteen steps leading up to the chancel. The chancel itself is curtained off and the action of the play takes place upon the two landings which break the eighteen steps. The exits and entrances are from the "Quire Doors" and the transepts. The characters are seven male spirits—The Power, The Sword, The Mercy, The Light, The Spirit of Christ, Peter, and Paul—; three conventional Wise Men and three quite unconventional Shepherds; Mary the Mother of Jesus; and a Chorus representing the Host of Heaven.

In the first part of the play the four angels—The Power, The Sword, The Mercy, and The Light—try to persuade The Spirit of Christ not to take man's body and go to earth. They warn him of the dangers: he may be overcome by fierce temptations; he may only bring suffering to others; men, being too cumbered with clay, will not receive him or his gospel. He replies that he must go to bring to men "the joy untold of knowledge of my Father and his Kingdom." They then press their opposition by foretelling what trouble, what bitter enmity, what failure he will experience, in order that, knowing to the utmost what he will face, he may "make choice whether to go or stay." His family and his friends will desert him; king, priest, and governor will turn against him; even the young will think him mad. Says the spirit called The Power:

>   Your followers
> Will dwindle to a few, of whom some three
> Will know the beauty of your thought.
> You, knowing of your failure, will be tempted
> To doubt your spirit's mission, and despair.
> In agony, you will think that God forgets you.
> You will be Man, not Spirit, in Man's pain.
> Then, in a hurry, will come bonds and insult,
> False witness, cruelty and ignominy,
> The wild beasts within men yelling for blood;
> You who would save Mankind will be held fast
> And nailed upon a cross, where you will think:
> "Death with this hell of pain may quench the soul." [6]

[6] This and subsequent quotations are from *The Coming of Christ* by John Masefield (London and New York: The Macmillan Co., 1928). Used by special permission of Mr. Masefield.

The other spirits take on where The Power leaves off, reminding him of the beauty and peace of Heaven in contrast to the
ugliness and warfare of earth. It were better to

> Leave Man to perish.
> He is but Dust of Death upon the way
> Passed by our bright Eternities.

But the Spirit of Christ is resolute. He believes, in spite of the
truth of all they utter, that his coming to earth might "light a
way for men from earth's unhappiness to very God." Will they
not, then, grant him comfort in his going? The Power replies:

> We have no comfort: for your task will bring none.
> This we may say, that, after those three souls,
> Not one, of all, will understand your teaching.
> For you may mourn, but no one will lament,
> And pipe, yet no one dance.

The Spirit of Christ answers:

> So be it, then.
> But the attempt, being worthy, should be made.
> Having beheld Man's misery, sin and death,
> Not to go were treason.

The spirits of Peter and Paul appear and tell him more of
what he may expect including Peter's denial and Paul's persecution of him. But when he hears that in the end they will turn
to him, drink his cup, and die for his cause he announces that
his choice is gladly made, cost what it may in pain and cruelty.

> I lay aside my glory and my power
> To take up Manhood. . . .
> Though Hell itself assail: God will protect. . . .
> O brother Man, I come; hate me not always.

The next movement presents the coming of the Wise Men and the Shepherds to Bethlehem. The Wise Men are traditional; the Shepherds uniquely untraditional. These shepherds are not the ones we saw in Sunday School pageants in our childhood. Masefield drew not only upon his imagination but upon his own experiences as a farm hand. Instead of being pious herdsmen talking wistfully of a coming Saviour, they are very human, ignorant, and superstitious peasants complaining bitterly of the bleak weather, their long hours and low wages, and damning the rich. "What we want," says one, "is a good revolution. . . . Let us have a turn at the fire, the rich have a turn at the fold." And again, "It's time the workers should command and have the wealth they make. We are the ones who till the land, and what we grow they take." So whipping up their grievances, the two younger ones decide they will wait until the oldest shepherd goes to sleep, then they will slip off to the inn and have a drink, and next week they will steal a sheep and sell it. But the old one overhears them and takes them roundly to task. This only makes them defiant and they vent their spleen upon him and his talk about God and the government of men. "This talk of God is used by Kings and priests to frighten people . . . to scare them so as to make them easier to govern." In the midst of their quarrel about the existence or non-existence of a God who cares anything for them bursts the vision of the angelic host singing its good tidings of peace on earth, good will among men.

Quickly now the play reaches its climax in the scene of Mary and the Child in the stable at Bethlehem with the three kings offering their royal gifts, the wondering shepherds their humble ones, and the choir singing its angelic welcome.

This prosy summary of the action does violence to the play as a whole, for it omits the beauty of Masefield's poetry and

the spiritual lift of the music by Gustav Holst. But it may
suggest the difference between Masefield's treatment of the
story and that of the amateur writer of a Nativity drama.
Masefield presents the coming of Christ against the black background of a suffering and warring world filled with hatred.
The ordinary Nativity play shows no black background, but
only an idyllic scene of gentle peasants and peaceful times. He
is concerned with the *need* of a Saviour and a new way of life;
the traditional Nativity is concerned with a supernatural mani-
festation without the need for it. Masefield brings to his play
the basic elements of dramatic interest which Aeschylus and
the other Greek dramatists discovered and utilized: characters
in conflict, a struggle familiar to everyone, suspense, climax,
choice, and deep emotion. These are notably absent in most
modern Nativities. Incidentally he was severely criticized for
the earthy dialogue of his shepherds. He replied (I am told)
that to make them convincing as shepherds he had to choose
between having them talk about their hard times and the need
of a revolution or about the hoof-and-mouth disease, and the
former seemed the more fitting.

The life of Jesus has a strong fascination for him. He has
written three other plays around it—*Good Friday, Easter,* and
The Trial of Jesus.[7] In all of them, with a fresh and vigorous
imaginative power he seeks to present the timeless and univer-

[7] Of these, *The Trial of Jesus* is the only full-length drama. It was
written for private production in Masefield's country home, Boar's Hill,
where it was first presented to a distinguished audience on May 9, 1925.
It centers, as the title indicates, around Jesus and his two trials before
Pilate. Jesus himself appears upon the stage—a fact which precluded
production in an English theatre since the regulations of the English
censor forbid the representation of divine characters. The play is set in a
framework of Greek tragedy beginning with a prayer and a choric prologue and using choric interludes between the scenes and acts. It is
entirely in prose except for these choruses. It has not been produced in
the American theatre but is available in book form (Macmillan, 1925).

sal elements in the immortal tragedy. "Tragedy," he once wrote, "at its best is a vision of the heart of life. The heart of life can only be laid bare in the agony and exaltation of dreadful acts. The vision of agony, or spiritual contest, pushed beyond the limits of dying personality, is exalting and cleansing. It is only by such vision that a multitude can be brought to the passionate knowledge of things exalting and eternal." Clearly the poet who consecrates his pen to such a purpose manifests the influence of Christ in his life and in his dramas.

EMLYN WILLIAMS

For the last of our modern English dramas in this study, let us examine a play by one of the younger men whose work shows high promise—Emlyn Williams. He has come up the hard way—from a coal mine in Wales to odd jobs in a theatre, then to acting and writing. He is in his thirties but has already written several plays including *Night Must Fall, Morning Star, Light of Heart, He was Born Gay,* and *The Corn Is Green.* Of these we shall deal only with *The Corn Is Green* which most of us have probably seen either in the stage version starring Ethel Barrymore or in the motion picture version starring Bette Davis. In an article in the *New York Times* Williams has told us how he came to write it. It was just after the failure of an earlier play which the critics lambasted, calling it "sentimental claptrap." That phrase got under his skin. He would wait a while—several hours anyway—and then write a new play, one at which no critic could hurl that damning epithet. His wife suggests that he might write it around his boyhood schoolteacher in Wales—a Miss Cooke. He had intended some day to write a novel about her—but a play? It seemed preposterous at first but the more he thought of that middle-aged, austere but devoted schoolmarm, the more the idea intrigued him. Certainly no one could call such a play "sentimental clap-trap." Soon his typewriter began to click. When he had finished the drama, some months later, he sent it to Miss Cooke, asking her if she had any objections. She replied with a characteristically laconic telegram: "No objections, but can't see anyone being interested."

The action centers around the struggle of this teacher—Miss Moffat in the play—to establish a school for the underprivileged people of a small Welsh mining village. The village is owned by a beef-headed English squire who heartily disapproves her whole project, and comes to say so after her school has been going about six weeks. What's the good of it? Mining coal is the business of these people; they don't need education for that. It might give them ideas, make them dissatisfied and dangerous. He gives them all they need—a hamper at Christmas for every family, a whopping tankard of beer on his birthday—and he is "not going to have any of this damned hanky-panky in his village." He will see to it that she won't be able to get any building—not even a barn—for her school. Why doesn't she take up croquet and keep herself out of mischief? The language in which she replies to the squire is certainly not the language any genteel croquet player would use:

"I should just like to point out that there is a considerable amount of dirt, ignorance, misery and discontent abroad in this world, and that a good deal of it is due to people like you, because you are a stupid, conceited, greedy, good-for-nothing, addle-headed nincompoop, and you can go to blue blazes. Good night!" [8]

[8] Emlyn Williams, *The Corn Is Green*. Random House, 1941. This, and subsequent quotations from the play, used by permission.

The squire's opposition is but one of several difficulties that have thwarted her. Chief among them is the apathy of the young miners themselves. A few have enrolled as a lark but they are almost illiterate and without ambition. She is discouraged and about ready to quit. But that same evening she reads over some exercise books the pupils have handed in. One of them stands out above the rest. Its grammar is bizarre and its spelling entirely original but a few words and phrases in it glow with feeling. "The mine is dark. . . . If a light come in the mine . . . I can touch with my hands the leaves of the trees, and underneath where the corn is green. . . ." That glow might be fanned into a flame. She talks with the boy who wrote the essay—Morgan Evans, an orphan whose father and brothers had been killed in a mine accident. He is fifteen years old, quick, impudent, and combative, but he warms to her appreciation. Her discouragement vanishes. She may not be able to educate the whole village, but if she can make something of this one boy her work will not have been in vain. She will stick. The squire can go to blue blazes.

From this moment she concentrates her best efforts upon developing the mind and spirit of Morgan Evans. She carries on with the rest of the school, of course, but the success or failure of this gamble of her life among the miners depends upon her success or failure with him. The odds are against her. His habits of speech, thought, and behavior have already been molded by the rough conditions of his work in the mines and the wretched associations of the village pub. Moreover, he has his own battles to fight. The other boys of the mine jeer at him when he begins to use language better than their own. Like them, he drinks and when under the influence of liquor the worst in him comes out: he is passionate, quarrelsome, and rebellious. Occasionally he flares up at her and she may well wonder whether anyone can make a silk purse out of a sow's ear. But her patience persists and her hope brightens as the months pass and the boy's mind begins to stretch toward new horizons.

At the end of two years, during which she has surmounted or muddled through various obstacles, she conceives the idea of having him try for an entrance scholarship to Oxford University, one of the few granted by a series of competitive examinations. It will mean that she must first find a sponsor for him—a patron. No one in the village could fill the requirements but the squire who has been so hostile to her work. In a memorable scene she seeks to persuade the squire. He could have understood backing a race horse, but a Welsh miner to become a scholar—preposterous! Miss Moffat plays delicately upon his vanity, reminding him of the honor that came to Lord Bolingbroke who served as patron for Alexander Pope, and to the Earl of Southampton as patron for William Shakespeare. By such arguments, coupled with a surprising amount of feminine charm, she wins over the squire.

Exultant, she breaks the news to Morgan Evans, but at the wrong moment. He has been drinking and the devil of rebellion is dominant within him. He will have nothing to do with the idea. He doesn't want to go to Oxford and be a gentleman. He has had too much schooling already. His miner friends have begun to call him "the schoolmistress's little dog." He accuses her of having no interest in him except to make him a machine to do her bidding. He will have no more of it. He will go back to the mines. Hurt and angry as she is, she makes the worst possible reply. She indulges in self-pity, reminding him of all she had done for him these two years and charging him with ingratitude. This only inflames him and he rejoins that he doesn't want to be thankful to any strange woman. Her heart is near to breaking.

After this agonizing scene Morgan is an easy victim for a little wench named Bessie who, in revenge for discipline Miss Moffat had imposed upon her, had determined to strike back at her by seducing this teacher's pet. She succeeds. Luckily Miss Moffat learns nothing of it. Next day, sobered and a bit ashamed, Morgan is back at school. With renewed hope and vigor she sets to work to teach him Greek, although she knows little of it herself and is put to it to keep a jump ahead of him. So the weeks pass and the day of the preliminary examination draws near.

On the morning when Morgan is to take it, the little wench, Bessie, who has been away, returns and announces to Miss Moffat that it's no good having Morgan sit for the examinations. He won't be going to Oxford even if he wins, for he is the father of the baby she is to bear and he will have to marry her. Miss Moffat must protect Morgan from hearing of this at such a critical moment. Threatening violence to Bessie if she blabs to anybody before they can have a talk she manages to get the girl out of the room. A few moments later Morgan sits down at the desk unaware of the threat that hangs over him and begins the preliminary examination.

Seven months later, as the last act begins, the whole village awaits excitedly the news of the results of Morgan's final examinations for the scholarship. The people had seen him off to take them and now he is due back. The pressures upon Miss Moffat's heart and nervous system have become intense. Has her protege won or lost? What has happened to Bessie whom she had sent away and kept silent thus far? If Morgan has won and then hears of Bessie's child—and his—what will it do to him and his future? If he has lost——?

She has not long to wait. Morgan arrives, but does not yet know the result of the examinations; it will be telegraphed. He thinks he has lost, for, among other things, he spent five minutes explaining why St. Paul sailed from a town three hundred miles inland. But he has had a soul-lifting experience, and he is exuberant as he describes it to Miss Moffat.

"I have come back—from the world! Since the day I was born, I have been a prisoner behind a stone wall, and now somebody has given me a leg-up to have a look at the other side . . . they cannot drag me back again, they cannot, they *must* give me a push and send me over!"

Miss Moffat thinks if three days at Oxford had so stimulated him, what would three years do? He had been among educated men and for the first time in his life had carried on long conversations with them. He tells her that all the thoughts she had given him and that had been locked up in his head as if they were useless had come pouring out in those conversations. Walking back to his room in the moonlight after one of them he had seen and understood what she had been doing for him.

"Everything I have ever learnt from these books, and from you, was lighted up—like a magic lantern—ancient Rome, Greece, Shakespeare, Carlyle, Milton . . . everything had a meaning, because I was in a new world—my world! And so it came to me why you had worked like a slave to make me ready for this scholarship."

A few moments later, while Morgan is out of the room, Bessie arrives, completely changed—her hair up, smartly dressed, and flashily pretty in a cheap, opulent fashion. She announces that four weeks earlier she had given birth to a baby boy and has now come to demand that Morgan marry her and give the baby his name. No arguments avail. Miss Moffat, in an agony of fear and resentment, questions Bessie. Had Morgan known of the child's coming? No. What had Bessie been doing in these months? Having a good time. She has had several gentlemen friends and especially one at the moment who would like to marry her but he won't take the child. " 'E says it would be different if the father had been a pal of his," Bessie reports. She knows Morgan "will do the right thing" out of his sense of chivalry—and the whole village will insist upon it.

Here is the crisis that breaks open Miss Moffat. If Morgan marries the girl there will be no Oxford for him. He will ultimately go back to the mines, start drinking again, and his future will be blacked out. Her own labors will have come to nought. What to do? When all other possibilities have been canvassed there seems but one solution: she must adopt the child. It is a bitter choice, but she makes it on condition that Bessie will clear out, marry her gentleman swell, and never let Morgan know of the whole affair. Bessie agrees and goes.

But the end is not yet. The squire has heard of Bessie's baby and of Morgan's part and tells the boy of it. Morgan promptly decides that he will "do the only thing any fellow with guts in him must do"—marry the girl. He will not hear of Miss Moffat's adopting the baby; it is his responsibility and his alone. At this juncture a telegram arrives, announcing that Morgan Evans has won the scholarship. The village prepares to celebrate. There is no time to lose. Miss Moffat is alone with Morgan and she goes about the business of battering down his resolution to marry the girl. He has a larger duty. No, not to her, but to the world. She wants him to be a writer and to make his writing serve humanity. "You have brains, shrewdness, eloquence, and imagination; and Oxford will give you enough of the graces."

MORGAN: For what?
MISS MOFFAT: Maybe to become a great man of our country. "If a light come in the mine" you said, remember?
MORGAN: Yes.
MISS MOFFAT: Make that light come in the mine and some day free these children. And you could do more, much, much more; you could be a man for a future nation to be proud of.

He responds to her appeal and consents at last to her sacrifice for him. It is more than the adoption of the child and the years of its care that she is undertaking. She is never going to see him again, for "it would be madness" for him to come into contact with the child; so he must never come to see her. Outside, the celebration has begun. Morgan goes to receive the honors. Miss Moffat announces school as usual tomorrow at nine o'clock.

We have come a long way from Shakespeare and have no thought of comparing this recent drama with one of his masterpieces. In majesty of scope, beauty of line, profundity of character study, and epic surge of rhythm there is no comparison. But for all that, if Shakespeare were alive in this day when democracies are on the march and the last of the monarchies tottering to their fall, he might well be cheering the young playwrights like Emlyn Williams for dramatizing the humble heroes of the democratic way of life. Miss Moffat is a worthy symbol of them.

Leaving to the dramatic critics an appraisal of Mr. Williams' art, let us turn to our particular concern. Is there here any evidence of the influence of Christ? Suppose we apply our three criteria. First, the central character—at the moment of her crisis when she has to choose between allowing Morgan to give up his career and having him go on with it through her sacrificial adoption of his child and never seeing him again, what does her choice reveal about her religion? She sacrifices herself not simply for one she loves but for the larger good he may do in the future for the underprivileged children of the mines. It is a choice that one would expect from a woman who had consecrated her life to bringing deliverance to captives, recovery of sight to the blind, and healing to them that are bruised.

Second, the spiritual insight of the author—in the play as a whole are the spiritual insights he reveals in harmony with those of Jesus? There are many spiritual insights in the life and teaching of Jesus, but probably none greater than this: that those who follow his way of life must sooner or later bear a cross. It is the vicarious suffering of the innocent for the guilty, and it has redeeming power. At the climax of Miss Moffat's long labor of love for Morgan Evans she bears a cross.

Third, the total effect of the play upon the audience—does it send the audience away exalted in spirit with a deepened sense of fellowship with God and man? Perhaps not directly with God, but certainly with the very human characters whose souls are mirrored in this drama. And who can spend these two hours with Miss Moffat without feeling exalted that there are such teachers and social workers living in the obscure places of the earth as daily witnesses to the potential dignity of human life?

CHAPTER V

Modern American Drama

WE HAVE seen that the drama, in its history in occidental civilizations, has usually passed through these phases: an origin in worship, a development into an art which seeks to interpret life, a decline into an amusement which seeks escape from life, a "show business" conducted for revenue only, and finally a period of repression and censorship. In America, which inherited its early culture from England and Europe, drama began in the show business phase, for that was the phase of English and Continental drama of the nineteenth century. Our first plays in this country were borrowings from abroad. Such original dramas as appeared were imitations of sentimental British comedies and melodramas. They were produced in the public rooms of taverns, in town halls, and wherever a platform, a couple of hundred chairs, and a box office might be available. Especially the box office. American drama, for the most part, is still in the show business phase. The box office still dominates. Whether the drama as an art can survive the theatre as a business—and particularly a business controlled largely by speculators who want to get rich quick—is an open question.

As American culture has developed and our native dramatists have tried to interpret our deeper insights and higher aspirations, various attempts have been made to rescue the art of drama from the deadening effects of the commercialism of the theatre. A generation ago the Little Theatre movement was started. Local stock companies and civic repertory theatres sprang up in scores of cities and in some rural districts. They fought a valiant battle. Eva LeGallienne in New York, Thomas Wood Stevens in Chicago, Jessie Bonstelle in Detroit, Gilmore Brown in Pasadena, Glenn Hughes in Seattle, and Alfred G. Arnold in North Dakota pioneered in this movement. These and scores of others with the same high purposes struggled through lean years on shoe-string budgets and with limited public support. Then came the Great Depression. For four years, from 1935 to 1939, Mrs. Hallie Flanagan of Vassar College made a heroic effort to found a National Theatre to gather up and consolidate the work of thousands of native dramatists, actors and directors throughout the country under the ægis of the Federal Theatre Project. It was to be a people's theatre with the best seats at fifty-five cents and producing centers in leading cities from Maine to California. It gave employment to a multitude of young artists and produced some notable plays to appreciative audiences. But the Dies Committee thought it smacked of communism and Congress suddenly cut off its appropriation. Since then Mr. Lucre and his mercenary crew have practically dominated the American theatre. Most of the dramas produced outside of the commercial theatres of a few large cities have been done by colleges, high schools, and churches.

Nevertheless, our leading dramatists have worked within the commercial theatre as best they could in spite of its cramping limitations. The Theatre Guild, The Group Theatre, The Playwrights' Theatre, The Labor Theatre and a few lesser organizations, together with the more sagacious of the commercial producers, have provided stages where many young playwrights have found opportunity to interpret life as they saw it. As a result America, in the last quarter century, has produced a rather bumper crop of dramatists including Maxwell Anderson, Philip Barry, S. N. Behrman, Marc Connelly, Rachel Crothers, Paul Green, Lillian Hellman, Sidney Howard, Sidney Kingsley, George Kaufman, Emmet Lavery, Clifford Odets, Elmer Rice, William Saroyan, Irwin Shaw, Robert Sherwood, John Steinbeck and Thornton Wilder. Probably not more than one in four of their plays becomes a box-office success, but a higher proportion will be remembered long after many box-office successes have been forgotten.

Since in our limited space we cannot deal with all these dramatists, I have selected certain plays of O'Neill, Connelly and Wilder for our study here. Before discussing them, however, let us give brief attention to a few plays by others who have also evidenced a deeper-than-ordinary interest in man's spiritual struggles. Certainly this could be said of Maxwell Anderson. In his *Winterset* he dramatizes the spiritual torment caused in half a dozen lives when legal justice miscarries as it did in the Sacco-Vanzetti case. In this and his other plays he manifests a strong passion for social justice and democracy, and for America as the country where they should be realized. In *Valley Forge* he pictures the hard-bitten soldiers in the crisis that tested Washington's faith and theirs in the American dream. In *Journey to Jerusalem* he goes deeper yet into the origins of the age-long struggle for man's redemption from tyranny of body and soul and finds it in the faith in God that kindled the mind of the boy Jesus. In his essay, "Prelude to Poetry in the Theatre," he expresses eloquently his conviction that "the stage is still a cathedral" and that "the theatre, more than any other art, has the power to weld and determine what the race dreams into what the race will become."

Philip Barry has concerned himself mostly with sensitive and well-to-do individuals caught in the emotional tangles of unhappy marriages, or rebelling against the money-mindedness of our materialistic society. His deftness in characterization, and his gifts for comedy and scintillating dialogue, are superlative; but he seldom penetrates to the deeper springs of action in religion. Exceptions are his *John,* a powerful portrait of John the Baptist, and *Here Come the Clowns,* a prophetic cry in the modern wilderness of cynicism and a vigorous—if somewhat cloudy—affirmation of faith in God and man.

Rachel Crothers' *Susan and God* topped her long list of successful comedies about women. It is a delightful story of a flighty and self-centered woman who, in middle age, becomes a convert to Christianity during a revival such as that initiated by the Oxford Group Movement. It seemed to promise her a new and pleasant sensation. But she soon finds that it costs her dearly in ease and comfort with its demands that she devote herself seriously to her alcoholic husband and her neglected daughter. In the end she pays the price and the family takes a fresh start. But one may question whether this woman, so unstable in her emotions and superficial in her thinking, will not soon join the next popular movement that comes along.

Paul Green's *In Abraham's Bosom* presents a tragic story of a Negro educator's virtual crucifixion on a cross of white man's prejudice and Negro inertia. His *Johnny Johnson,* a musical fantasy, tells a similar tale of a sincere pacifist in conflict with an idiotic world hell-bent for war's destruction.

In *Dead End,* Sidney Kingsley, with genuine compassion but without a line of preaching, portrays so convincingly the evil effects of slum life on children that the audience wants to do something about it. In *The Patriots* he dramatizes the great conflict between Thomas Jefferson and Alexander Hamilton—a conflict still raging wherever democracy has leaders of courage and vision.

Curiously enough the only passion play written for the modern American theatre has come from the pen of a writer of humorous verse and short stories—Don Marquis. His *Dark Hours* is a reverent and poignant play about the trial and crucifixion of Jesus. (It was written during the dark hours of Mr. Marquis' personal tragedy when he lost his wife and his little son.)

The Family Portrait, by Lenore Coffee and William Joyce Cowen, is a quiet and memorable play although it hardly achieves the stature of great drama. In conversational English it tells reverently and with tenderness the story of Jesus as his mother and brothers may have seen him. Jesus himself does not appear upon the stage, but he is the central character. His mother comes nearest to understanding him and she must constantly defend him against his impatient brothers. They are trying to make a go of their carpenter shop in Nazareth and resent his running off on preaching expeditions. When his preaching becomes popular and makes the family name famous, they are pleased: it helps business. But when Jesus gets himself involved in a political struggle with their leading customers and is finally crucified, they regard it as a family disgrace and try to forget him. But Mary remembers, and cherishes the memory. At the end of the play she is persuading Judah, another son, to name his firstborn after Jesus. "It's a nice name," she says, "I'd like him not to be forgotten." (Where is there a more moving last line?)

Other plays of religious significance by these and other American playwrights will be found, listed under their names, in the Appendix. And now let us take up in somewhat more detail a study of some of the plays of O'Neill, Connelly, and Wilder.

EUGENE O'NEILL

Born in New York in 1888, son of an actor, O'Neill received his early education in a number of schools and later entered Princeton University, where the authorities did not permit him to stay long. For the next dozen years he was a migrant laborer—at least he was a migrant and worked at such varied occupations as seaman, assistant manager of a theatrical company, prospector for gold in Spanish Honduras, clerk in the draughting department of an electrical company, assistant in the office of the Singer Sewing Machine Company at Buenos Aires, mule tender on a cattle steamer, actor, and reporter. This knocking about the Western Hemisphere ended with a case of weak lungs and a six-month rest period in a sanatorium. While there the urge to write came to him. Within a year he had completed his first play—*The Web*. At twenty-six he studied for a year at Harvard in Professor George Pierce Baker's famous 47 Workshop. At twenty-eight he spent a summer at Provincetown where the Provincetown Players began to produce some short plays he had written. Then came his long play, *Beyond the Horizon,* and his career as a leader in American drama was launched. Since then he has written some fifty plays and heroically destroyed eighteen of them. Among the best known of the thirty-two he allowed to survive are *Emperor Jones, Anna Christie, The Hairy Ape, The Great*

God Brown, Strange Interlude, Mourning Becomes Electra, Ah, Wilderness, and *Days Without End.* In 1936 he was awarded the Nobel Prize in Literature. Meanwhile an ever-lengthening shelf of books about his work and the development of his thought has become available for students of the modern drama.

For our purposes let us examine briefly two of his later plays—*Mourning Becomes Electra* and *Days Without End.*[1] The first is a nine-act drama, or more accurately, a trilogy of three plays done somewhat in the manner of the Greek tragedies, minus the chorus, and modeled after Euripides' version of the Electra story. The essential action in the Greek story included the murder of Agamemnon by his wife Clytemnestra, the avenging murder of Clytemnestra and her lover Aegisthus by Orestes and his sister Electra, and the resulting punishment, suffering, and ultimate pardon of Orestes. O'Neill puts the story in modern dress, saying frankly that he followed Euripides' version.

The action parallels the Greek original up to the moment of the climax when Electra and Orestes murder their mother. But here there is a significant difference between O'Neill and Euripides. The difference lies in the spiritual insight of the two authors. Earlier in this essay, it was pointed out that what a dramatist sees in a character, once he has broken open that character in the crisis, depends upon the dramatist's own spiritual insight. So it is here. The difference will be evident if we compare the reactions of Electra and Orestes of Euripides to the murder they have committed with the reactions of O'Neill's modern counterparts of those characters—Lavinia

[1] Quotations from these plays used by permission of the publishers, Random House, Inc.

and Orin—as they stand over the body of their mother whom they have driven to suicide.

EURIPIDES
Orestes.

O Dark of Earth, O God,
  Thou to whom all is plain;
Look on my sin, my blood,
  This horror of dead things
    twain:
Gathered as one they lie
Slain; and the slayer was I,
  I, to pay for my pain!

Electra.

Let tear rain upon tear,
  Brother: but mine is the
    blame.
A fire stood over her,
  And out of the fire I came,
I, in my misery . . .
And, I was the child at her
    knee
  'Mother' I named her name.

Orestes.

Apollo, alas for the hymn
  Thou sangest as hope in
    mine ear!
The Song was of Justice dim,
  But the Deed is anguish
    clear;
And the Gift, long nights of
    fear,

O'NEILL
Orin (Orestes).

You wanted Wilkins just as you wanted Brant!

Lavinia (Electra).

That's a lie!

Orin.

You're doing the lying! You know damned well that behind all your pretense about Mother's murder being an act of justice was your jealous hatred! She warned me of that and I see it clearly now! You wanted Brant for yourself!

Lavinia (*fiercely*).

It's a lie! I hated him!

Orin.

Yes, after you knew he was her lover! (*He chuckles with a sinister mockery*) But we'll let

Of blood and of wandering,
Where cometh no Greek
thing,
Nor sight, nor sound on the air.
Yea, and beyond, beyond,
Roaming—what rest is
there?
Who shall break bread with
me?
Who, that is clean, shall see
And hate not the blood-red
hand,
His mother's murderer?

Electra.

And I? What clime shall hold
My evil, or roof it above?
I cried for dancing of old,
I cried in my heart for love:
What dancing waiteth me
now?
What love that shall kiss my
brow
Nor blench as the brand
thereof?

Orestes.

Saw'st thou her raiment there,
Sister, there in the blood?
She drew it back as she stood,
She opened her bosom bare,
She bent her knees to the
earth,

that pass for the present—I
know it's the last thing you
could ever admit to yourself!—
and come to what I've written
about your adventures on my
lost islands. Or should I say,
Adam Brant's islands! He had
been there too, if you'll remember! Probably he'd lived
with one of the native women!
He was that kind! Were you
thinking of that when we were
there?

Lavinia (chokingly).

Stop it! I—I warn you—I
won't bear it much longer!

*Orin (as if he hadn't heard
—in the same sinister mock-
ing tone).* What a paradise
the Islands were for you,
eh? All those handsome men
staring at you and your strange
beautiful hair! It was then you
finally became pretty — like
Mother! You knew they all de-
sired you, didn't you? It filled

The knees that bent in my
birth . . .
And I . . . Oh, her hair, her
hair . . .
(*He breaks into inarticulate
weeping.*)

you with pride! Especially
Avahanni! You watched him
stare at your body through
your clothes, stripping you
naked! And you wanted him!

Thus Euripides, when he has broken open Orestes and Electra, sees in their souls not only torment and struggle but a cleansing repentance and a refining fire of suffering that combine to create tragic beauty. O'Neill sees in his characters a similar torment, but no repentance, no refining fire, and no beauty.

Both Euripides and O'Neill are dramatic craftsmen of the first order. But Euripides adds something to his skill—something that O'Neill does not have—a deep spiritual insight, a broad sympathy, and a strong faith in the ultimate goodness of the universe. It is that difference which distinguishes the artist whose work has survived twenty-four centuries from the craftsman whose works are admired now for their skill and power, but which do not possess those deeper spiritual qualities which endear them to the affections of mankind. And unless an artist can lay hold of the affections, it is doubtful if his work will be cherished from generation to generation.

This example seems fairly typical of Mr. O'Neill's dramas up to the year 1933. By that time he had become a master craftsman in dramatic construction. Probably no other playwright of modern times had developed a greater intensity of power in the portrayal of the crises in which his characters struggled. No other had so clearly revealed human souls naked, stripped of all pretense. But Mr. O'Neill seldom found beauty in the characters he portrayed. As he stood upon the brink and looked down into the crater of a soul he found only torment and selfishness. Seldom nobility; never divinity.

This is not to say that he found only dirt or triviality. He did not find much dirt, and very little triviality. He occasionally found some elements of greatness. But in the souls of his major characters, where he saw God and the Devil struggling against each other, he nearly always found the Devil winning out. He did not rejoice that the struggle issued in the Devil's favor—but that is what he saw and so he recorded it. Further, he saw that the Devil's victory meant the ultimate destruction of the soul. O'Neill was a stern moralist. Over and over again the fact that "the wages of sin is death" is illustrated in the lives of his characters. But never, until after 1933, did he discover that "the gift of God is eternal life." He seemed under the conviction that not a few of his characters were victims of predestination. They were foreordained to be damned. But if he had ever heard of the doctrines of grace and forgiveness he did not remember them when he looked into the souls of his characters.

Something happened to Eugene O'Neill between the writing of *Mourning Becomes Electra* and the writing of *Days Without End* three years later. What it was only he could tell. But whatever it was it had a deepening effect upon his spiritual insight, his sympathy, and his faith as we shall see.

In *Days Without End* O'Neill deals with the problem of soul-sickness. The central character is John Loving who has become a split personality. The two parts of his personality are played by two actors, dressed identically and always together upon the stage. One part—whom the other characters see—is that of a young business man who in his spare time is writing an autobiographical novel. He is sincere, affectionate to his wife, and rather wistful as he tries to work out a philosophy and a faith for life. The other part of him, invisible to everyone except the audience, wears a mask symbolic of the cynicism that dominates his soul. The two parts of this split personality react differently to the words and the acts of the other characters; sometimes it is the hopeful part that speaks, sometimes the cynical, with resulting complications in his social relationships.

How did John Loving come to have this split personality? What are the consequences of it? Is there a cure for it? We learn from a kindly old Priest—Father Baird—the story of John's youth. He had been the child of very religious parents whom he had loved with his whole heart. Their home atmosphere had surrounded John with affection and he had been happy in those boyhood days until his father died and his mother fell ill. In an agony of fear John had prayed that his mother might recover. But she sank lower and lower. Then he prayed for a miracle to save her, but no miracle had been granted. She died. Thereupon John renounced his faith and began a long search for some form of good life entirely outside of Christianity. First he had turned to atheism, then to socialism, next to anarchy, and later to communism. He had taken up each of these new faiths with all the zeal of a crusader, but none had held him long. Becoming disgusted with sociological nostrums, he had turned to the mysticism of the East and had been fascinated first by Lao-tze and then by the teachings of Buddha. Eventually these, too, paled and he turned again to western philosophy and worshiped at the shrine of the ancient Greeks. But he found no peace for his soul until he met Elsa, came to love her, and married her. In her, at last, his life seems to have found fulfillment.

For a few years Elsa and he are supremely happy, although it is a self-centered happiness and he has never settled the matter of his faith. He has no spiritual roots. Having tried various philosophies and religions and found them all wanting, he thinks he can get along without any. And so his cynical self develops subconsciously and is ready to take control of his life at the first crisis. The crisis comes one day when Elsa is absent and John is made the object of a seductive attack by another woman—Lucy—who wants to be revenged on her own faithless husband. John resists at first but his resistance weakens when his cynical self argues that a bit of adultery with this woman would be "an act as meaningless as that of one fly with another, and of equal importance to life." So the adultery is committed. All this John has put in his novel. And now he doesn't know how to end the story. His conscience torments him. The arguments between his cynical self refusing to make a fuss over nothing and his guilty self seeking forgiveness drive him nearly mad.

Here the plot of John's novel merges with the plot of O'Neill's play. John thinks his wife Elsa, although she is just recovering from an illness, will be able to help him finish the novel. He resolves to tell her the story of it and ask whether or not the wife would forgive the husband. Meanwhile, however, Elsa has had a call from her old friend Lucy, and Lucy, tormented by her own conscience, can't refrain from confessing that she has had a fleeting experiment with adultery although she doesn't tell Elsa that it was with John. Lucy bitterly regrets the whole episode and testifies that "as a love substitute or even a pleasurable diversion it's greatly overrated." Elsa is shocked but tries not to seem too prudish or to condemn Lucy too harshly. Later that evening, however, John is telling her the plot of his novel including the sin of his central character. The details are exactly those of Lucy's story and Elsa cannot escape the realization of the revolting truth. When John puts the question to her, would the wife forgive? she gives an emphatic No. A few minutes later she excuses herself on the plea of a headache. John thinks she is retiring to her room, but she goes out into a stormy night, thinly clad, and spends hours walking in the rain trying to calm the anguish of her heart. When she returns, drenched, she is desperately ill, her body shaken with chills and burning with fever. John is frantic with worry over her condition. Where has she been, and why had she gone out at all? Elsa will have none of his tenderness. She tells him that she knows the truth—and she wants to die.

Thus far—and we are at the end of the third act—O'Neill has given us an honest picture of the effect of sin in human life. The sin of John and Lucy has not only made them miserable, it has reached out and struck down the happiness and faith of Elsa. It has smashed her home and cast her into hell. Here, if he had travelled no further in his thought than in earlier years, he would have dropped the final curtain. The wages of sin is death—what more is there to say?

Much more. And O'Neill adds a fourth act to tell it. In the first scene of this act we see John, haggard and worn, watching Elsa as in delirium she enters the crisis of pneumonia. He begs her forgiveness, although his cynical self, standing near him like a malignant shadow, jeers at him and tells him Elsa is going to die and there's nothing for him to do but make the best of it. The old priest urges John to pray. "It is only God," he says, "who can open her heart to forgiveness and give her back the will to live! Pray for His forgiveness, and He will have compassion on you! Pray to Him who is Love, who is infinite Tenderness and Pity!" John half-slips to his knees, repeating longingly, "Who is Love! If I could only believe again!" But his cynical self suddenly jerks him to his feet, reminding him that he had once prayed for his mother's recovery, and in vain. Let God prove to him that His love exists and then he will believe. The priest warns him that he may not bargain with God. Will he not make haste, before it is too late, to go to the church and at the foot of the cross to seek the grace of faith again? Torn by fear and grief, John ultimately goes out into the night, but whether to the church or to kill himself we are not sure. Seeing him go in such distress of soul, Elsa is moved to understanding and pity. Faintly she calls after him, "John! Come back! I'll forgive!" But he does not hear her.

In the final scene we find him in the old church and at the foot of the cross in a mortal struggle with his cynical self and praying that he may once more believe in God's love. His prayer is utterly unique in O'Neill's writings:

O Son of Man, I am Thou and Thou art I. Why hast Thou forsaken me? O Brother who lived and loved and suffered and died with us, who knowest the tortured hearts of men, canst Thou not forgive—now—when I surrender all to Thee—when I have forgiven Thee—the love that Thou once took from me?

His cynical self protests bitterly, but John's eyes, fixed upon the face of the Crucified, suddenly light up and he prays on in a voice that trembles with hope,

Ah! Thou hast heard me at last! Thou hast not forsaken me! Thou hast always loved me! I am forgiven! I can forgive myself —through Thee. I can believe! . . . At last I see! I have always loved! O Lord of Love, forgive Thy poor blind fool! . . . Thou art the Way—the Truth—the Resurrection and the Life, and he that believeth in Thy Love, his love shall never die!

As his prayer ends the cynical self falls dead. The sick soul of John Loving is no longer split; it is re-integrated through faith and love. The priest arrives and tells him that Elsa will live. John doesn't need the message—his love has already told him.

O'Neill, in this play, for the first time had realized that "the wages of sin is death" is but half the biblical sentence and that the other half is equally true: "but the gift of God is eternal life through Jesus Christ our Lord" (Romans 6:23). The play was rejected by Broadway.

Twelve years passed before the public saw a new play from O'Neill's pen. Then, in October, 1946, The Theatre Guild presented his four hour drama, *The Iceman Cometh,* written in 1939. It portrays some eighteen drunks and street walkers, habitués of a cheap Raines Law Hotel and ginmill in the year 1912. Each of these human wrecks lives on his "pipe dream"; that is, his illusion that he is only temporarily stranded and tomorrow will see him sailing happy seas again. Challenged by one of the characters to put this pipe dream to a test, each in turn sallies forth—only to return a little later, more broken than ever, to his alcohol and to cherishing what is left of his dream until the Iceman (Death) ends it all. Obviously in this play O'Neill has reverted to his pessimism. The fire of Christian faith which burned in *Days Without End* he has allowed to flicker down, if not out. Life, as he sees it in *The Iceman Cometh,* is not only sordid but hateful and without worth or dignity. Whatever the strength or weakness of the play as a piece of dramatic craftsmanship, its underlying philosophy reveals no influence of Christ.

MARC CONNELLY

The crash of the stock market in 1929 brought to a sudden end a decade of financial expansion which had no adequate roots in the general welfare of the people. The great depression followed with mounting unemployment, mortgages foreclosed on farms and urban homes, and with apple-stands manned by disillusioned veterans who had fought World War I "to make the world safe for democracy." The subsequent lean years were bad enough for all enterprises and the theatre suffered economically as much as others. But the real artists of the theatre did as real artists always do in times of distress: they sought to interpret the immediate miseries of life in the light of man's spiritual experience through the centuries. Looking back over the product of the serious playwrights of these years John Gassner has written: "The fact is that the thirties in America witnessed a period of drama equal in quality to the work of the preceding decade. The period has been rightly described by the sagacious critic John Mason Brown as 'these full lean years.'"

Probably no play did more to dramatize the most relevant of man's spiritual struggles of the past than Marc Connelly's *Green Pastures*.[2] Produced just after the crash in 1929, when speculators and others were jumping out the windows of skyscrapers and men and women everywhere felt confused and frustrated, this play brought healing and faith to troubled

[2] Quotations from this play used by permission of the publishers, Rinehart and Company.

souls. Moreover it performed its ministry with such grace of humor and imagination that it sent audiences back into the darkness of the world with laughter on their lips and sparkle in their eyes.

Mr. Connelly was born in McKeesport, Pennsylvania, in 1890. After graduation from Trinity Hall, Washington, Pennsylvania, he became a reporter on the *Pittsburgh Sun* and later on the *Dispatch* and the *Gazette Times* of the same city. His talent for humorous writing developing, he composed lyrics for a musical comedy. This took him to New York. The musical failed but he stayed on in New York as a free lance contributing to newspapers and magazines and doing occasional skits for revues. In 1921 he teamed up with George Kaufman and collaborated with him in writing a series of highly successful comedies—*Dulcy, To the Ladies, Merton of the Movies, Beggar on Horseback,* and others.

In 1924 the partnership was dissolved by mutual agreement and Mr. Connelly turned to more serious themes, but still with a light touch. He wrote *The Wisdom Tooth,* a fantasy which lingers happily, and a bit poignantly, in the memories of many who saw it. Its story centers around a young clerk— Bemis—who is brought to a sudden crisis when his sweetheart rejects him because he seems to have no courage, no mind of his own, and has become only a yes-man like thousands of other clerks in big establishments. He realizes the truth of her indictment. In a dream he re-lives his boyhood, visits his grandparents and catches some of their pioneer spirit, sees his own early ambition, his struggles, and the great day when he licked the town bully. Awaking, he resolves that the boy-he-used-to-be was more of a man than the clerk he now is, and that it is high time that he reassert the courage of his forebears and his youth. He faces his employer, denounces him for his unjust treatment of a stenographer and—gets fired himself. But he has a new self-respect and has re-won the admiration and faith of his sweetheart.

Three years later Mr. Connelly wrote the play that does for the human race what Bemis' excursion into his small-town past did for him. *The Green Pastures* Mr. Connelly calls a "fable suggested by Roark Bradford's southern sketches, 'Ol' Man Adam an' His Chillun.' " But it goes far beyond Mr. Bradford's charming sketches both in purpose and in nobility of plan. For it is nothing less than a dramatization of the spiritual essence of the Bible distilled through imagination of the Negro race. Its story is well known but it may be well to refresh the memory of its major scenes and characters. We are introduced first to ten children and an elderly preacher in the midst of a Sunday School class in the corner of a Negro church in a lower Louisiana town. The preacher—Mr. Deshee—is trying to make clear "de meat an' substance of de first five chapters of Genesis." The children raise questions about the Creation. For example, "What de worl' look like when de Lawd begin?" "How'd he git de idea he wanted it?" and, "Who was in N'Orleans den?" Mr. Deshee takes refuge in common sense spiced with imagination. "De answer is dat de Book ain't got time to go into all de details. . . . De Lawd expects us to figure out some things for ourselves." The scenes that follow are the "figuring out" as it went on in the resourceful mind of the old minister.

They began in a pre-creation Heaven where happy Negro angels wearing highly colored robes are enjoying a fish fry. They sing old-time spirituals and chat proudly of their sinlessness and their freedom from temptation. "If a lady wants a little constitutional she kin fly 'til she wing-weary without gittin' insulted." Into this gay party comes the archangel Gabriel heralding a visit from "de Lawd." "Gangway!" he cries, "Gangway for de Lawd God Jehovah!" (In all the history of drama has there ever been such a breath-taking announcement as this? Or an entrance more commanding of awe and wonder?) A reverent hush falls upon the angels and God enters. He is tall and dignified but not pompous; his face is kindly and his voice a rich bass. He is dressed as a Negro preacher would dress—in a long Prince Albert coat of black alpaca, black trousers, congress gaiters, white shirt and white bow tie. To the assembly of bowing angels he gravely puts questions: "Is you been baptized?" "Is you been redeemed?" "Do you bow mighty low?" To each of which they chant in unison, "Certainly, Lawd . . . Certainly, certainly, certainly, Lawd." Satisfied, he lifts his hand and breaks the spell of the divine formality. "Let de fish fry proceed," he says, and the angels resume their pleasures.

Before this scene is ended the character of "de Lawd" becomes clear. He is a very humane and generous God who loves his creatures and wants them to be happy. Moreover, he uses his creative power in making experiments. Discovering that the "biled custard" is tasteless because it lacks "firmament" he "passes a miracle" and creates such a deluge of "firmament" that the little cherubs are drenched to the skin and in danger of catching cold. What to do? There is no place in Heaven where the excess liquid can be drained off; so another miracle is required. "Dat's always de trouble wid miracles," he says. "When you pass one you always gotta r'ar back an' pass another . . . Let dere be a place to dreen off dis firmament. Let dere be mountains and valleys an' let dere be oceans and lakes . . . rivers and bayous to dreen it off in. As a matter of fac' let dere be de earth. An' when dat's done let dere be de sun, and let it come out and dry my cherubs' wings." Thus the earth is created. It is such a good earth, such "mighty nice farming country," especially "dat South forty" as Gabriel points out, that God is convinced he ought to have somebody to enjoy it. So he passes another miracle and creates Adam.

From here on the story of mankind unfolds following in the main the pattern of the biblical narrative but with the people all Negroes and their actions interpreted as an old Negro preacher understood them. We see Adam and Eve in the Garden of Eden and their first disobedience, Cain and the generations of his descendants given to murder and vice—a thoroughly bad lot, so bad that God is discouraged and deserts the human race for a few centuries. When next he returns to the earth he finds sin rampant. "Dis yere mankind I been peoplin' de earth wid sho' ain't much." He resolves to blot them out—all but Noah and his family, for he has found Noah a righteous man. So Noah is commanded to build the Ark, take aboard it his family and a male and female of every species of animal. (There is an unforgettable scene in which Noah pleads with God to be allowed to take two jugs of liquor aboard, but God insists that one is enough). The flood comes, man is destroyed, and after many days the waters recede, the animals and Noah and his family disembark, and God's second experiment with the human family begins. "I only hope it's goin' to work out all right," he sighs.

But it doesn't work out so. In a few centuries the new race of men is as bad as the old. God is troubled and greatly displeased. Gabriel wants to blow his horn and end the whole experiment. In fact Gabriel always carries his trumpet and is eager to use it. But God won't have it. To destroy the earth would be to admit failure of his creation. Man is "a kind of pet" of his and it wouldn't be right to give up trying to do something for him.

Here a new thought occurs. Perhaps the trouble has been that God has not let man help himself enough—to work out his own salvation, or at least work toward it. The trouble with Adam and Eve in the Garden of Eden was that they had nothing to do but enjoy themselves. Result: they got into mischief. "Man," says God, "ain't built jest to fool aroun' an' not do nothin'. Gabe, I'm gonter try a new scheme . . . Send in Abraham, Isaac an' Jacob."

The new scheme is that God will select a chosen group— the descendants of these men who had been among the few good citizens of earth—and develop them through one of their own leaders. So we have the scenes of the call of Moses, his interview with Pharaoh to demand that he release the Hebrew people from bondage—a demand backed up by the plagues on Egypt until Pharaoh consents. Then a scene, forty years later, at the end of the Exodus when the children of Israel enter the promised land under the leadership of Joshua as Moses, old and blind, is led up a hill by the hand of God into another promised land far more beautiful. Surely now the people have learned their lesson. They will live righteously in their new country and sin no more.

But in time even these chosen people turn away from God and his commandments. They worship gods of materialism and pleasure and eventually bring about their own downfall and become slave laborers in Babylon. God repents that he has made mankind and vows that he will deliver them no more. He has given them a good earth, he has sent them great leaders, prophets, warriors. He has provided just laws and commandments. But everything he has given has been defiled. Now he is tired of the struggle to make man worthy of the breath he has given him. He will deliver them no more.

Yet God cannot keep them out of his heart. Back in his heavenly office he is worried. He has withstood for hundreds of years the daily pleas of Abraham, Isaac, Jacob and Moses that he return to his chosen people. But two new factors have recently begun to bear upon him. One is the prophet Hosea who daily passes his door but never speaks and never seeks to enter. And every time Hosea passes the door God hears a voice from the earth, the voice of Hezdrel, one of the defenders of the besieged city of Jerusalem. God knows that Hezdrel and the last remnant of the defenders of that great city want help from him. But hasn't he vowed not to help any more? The voice of Hezdrel persists and finally God reluctantly relents and agrees to visit Hezdrel on earth, but not to give him any help. "I'm jest feelin' a little low, an' I'm only comin' down to make myself feel a little better, dat's all."

His talk with Hezdrel reveals God in a new light. He is a humble and a learning God—learning from his own creature. He does not tell Hezdrel who he is but identifies himself only as an old preacher from back in the hills. He learns that Hezdrel's bravery comes from his faith in Hosea's God of mercy, not from the old tribal God of wrath and vengeance. But are they not the same? Hezdrel doesn't know, but he is sure that the God of mercy is the only true God. And how did Hosea find out about this mercy? Hezdrel answers: "De only way he could find it. De only way I found it. De only way anyone kin find it . . . Through sufferin'." God thanks him and returns to heaven. There we behold him in the last scene, seated in an armchair and surrounded by the heavenly choir and other angels. This scene is a marvel of brevity and defies condensation.

GABRIEL: You look a little pensive, Lawd. (*God nods his head.*) Have a seegar, Lawd?

GOD: No, thanks, Gabriel. (*Gabriel goes to the table, accepts a cup of custard; chats with the angel behind the table for a moment as he sips, puts the cup down and returns to the side of God.*)

GABRIEL: You look awful pensive, Lawd. You been sittin' yere, lookin' dis way, an awful long time. Is it somethin' serious, Lawd?

GOD: Very serious, Gabriel.

GABRIEL: (*Awed by His tone.*) Lawd, is de time come for me to blow?

GOD: Not yet, Gabriel. I'm just thinkin'.

GABRIEL: What about, Lawd? (*Puts up hand. Singing stops.*)

GOD: 'Bout somethin' de boy tol' me. Somethin' 'bout Hosea, and himself. How dey foun' somethin'.

GABRIEL: What, Lawd?

GOD: Mercy. (*A pause.*) Through *sufferin'*, he said.

GABRIEL: Yes, Lawd.

GOD: I'm tryin' to find it, too. It's awful impo'tant. It's awful impo'tant to all de people on my earth. Did he mean dat even God must suffer? (*God continues to look out over the audience for a moment and then a look of surprise comes into his face. He sighs. In the distance a voice cries.*)

THE VOICE: Oh, look at him! Oh, look, dey goin' to make him carry it up dat high hill! Dey goin' to nail him to it! Oh, dat's a terrible burden for one man to carry!

(God rises and murmurs "Yes!" as if in recognition.
The heavenly beings have been watching him closely,
and now, seeing him smile gently, draw back, re-
lieved. All the angels burst into "Hallelujah, King
Jesus." God continues to smile as the lights fade
away. The singing becomes fortissimo.)

The influence of Christ upon the author and the content
of this play is obvious. With reverence and courage as well
as imagination Mr. Connelly has made God the central character and portrayed him as Christ preached him—a suffering
God, struggling against the evil in men and so loving them
that he gave his Son for their salvation. The spiritual insights
of the drama—from the results of sin stemming from man's
disobedience to the divine commands, to the hope of his redemption by way of love and the cross of sacrificial suffering—
are the insights of the Sermon on the Mount. The total effect
of the play, when reverently produced, has always been to send
the audience away exalted in spirit and with a deepened sense
of fellowship with God and man. It is probably the best-loved
play of the modern theatre.

THORNTON WILDER

To students of contemporary literature the works of Thornton Wilder are pure joy. A fresh breeze of spring, laden with
fragrance of blossoming fruit trees, blows through them. And
the breeze carries to the reader's mind and heart new hope
and the joy of living. The morbid fears, the dark delvings into
Freudian complexes, and the cynical outlook on man's nature
which have bedeviled the writings of lesser men, find no abid-

ing place in Mr. Wilder's novels and plays. They are swept away by the stronger winds of faith. Yet there is nothing of the Pollyanna about him. He is as conscious as any Barthian of the evil in the world and in the human heart. But he is also conscious of the beauty and he finds it in the commonplace as well as in the exalted experiences of life.

Someone has said of him that his favorite subject is the human soul and that all his works "deal with the mystery of death and judgment, the tragedy of beauty, and the pity of the ending of life's comedy." In his plays as well as his novels he seeks to bring the perspectives of eternity to the contemporary scene. That is what all great writers have sought, but few in recent literature have seemed aware that there are any perspectives of eternity. They remind one of the wayward Negro daughter whose mother said she "had a head full of momentary." Mr. Wilder's vision includes the "momentary," but sees it against the background of the long centuries past and to come.

Born in Madison, Wisconsin, his father the editor of the *Wisconsin State Journal,* he was taken at the age of nine to China where his father had been appointed United States Consul-General. His next eight years—perhaps the most impressionable of any boy's life—were spent among the imaginative Chinese. The influence of Chinese drama, which dispenses with properties with the exception of a few supplied by an ubiquitous property man, is clearly seen in the stage arrangements—or lack of them—of his play, *Our Town.* He prepared for college in California, had two years in Oberlin and, after two years in the Coast Artillery during World War I, graduated from Yale at twenty-three. William Lyon Phelps said that as an undergraduate Wilder was "unusually versatile, original and clever. He played and composed music, wrote much prose and verse, and stood well in his studies."

For the next seven years he was House Master and instructor in French at Lawrenceville School. He chose to teach French, we are told, so that he could wander as he wished in the paths of English Literature. He had gone on with his writing, experimenting with various forms and styles, but determined to write for pleasure rather than profit. The pleasure came, and the profit soon came tumbling after. His first novel, *The Cabala,* was published when he was twenty-eight, his Pulitzer-prize-winning novel *The Bridge of San Luis Rey* when he was thirty-one and ten years later his play *Our Town,* which also won the Pulitzer prize. Meanwhile he had written a charming collection of three-to-seven-minute plays, some of them distinctly religious, entitled *The Angel That Troubled the Waters* and another collection of one-act plays entitled *The Long Christmas Dinner.* Other works include his novels, *The Woman of Andros* and *Heaven's My Destination,* and his plays, *The Merchant of Yonkers* and *The Skin of Our Teeth.* Let us examine here *Our Town* [3] as representative of his dramatic writing.

The play dramatizes life in a New Hampshire village "with its humor and tragedy, its beauty and sordidness, set against a background of centuries of time, social history, and religious ideas." Although the scene is laid in New Hampshire and the characters have pronounced and delightful Yankee traits, their universal qualities shine through and touch the hearts of people who never saw New England. This may be due in part to the fact that the stage is bare; there is no

[3] Coward-McCan, publishers, 1938. Quotations by special permission of Mr. Wilder.

curtain, no scenery, and only a minimum of properties. Our imaginations fill in the background from our own memories of our home towns. The stage manager, standing at one side, provides a running commentary on the present, past, and future of the village and its inhabitants. Occasionally he acts a rôle himself.

The first act, called Daily Life, portrays the commonplace happenings of a single day in an ordinary village of 2600 population in the year 1901. We see it from dawn to bed-time at 9:30 o'clock. At breakfast we divide our attention between the family of Doc Gibbs, the village physician, and the family of Mr. Webb, the editor of the village paper. Mrs. Gibbs, in the midst of prodding her son George and her daughter Rebecca out of bed and down to breakfast, worries about her husband's not getting enough sleep and her son's being so interested in baseball he doesn't do his chores. Mrs. Webb worries less, but has her hands full with her daughter Emily (who admits she's the brightest girl in school) and with her son Wally who is also bright—when he's looking at his stamp collection.

Soon the school bell rings. Says Mrs. Webb: "Walk fast, but you don't have to run. Wally, pull up your pants at the knee. Stand up straight, Emily." Says Mrs. Gibbs: "You look real nice, Rebecca. Pick up your feet." The children are off to school and the two mothers gossip in neighborly fashion about their gardens and chickens and the amazing price which an antique dealer has offered for Mrs. Gibbs' old high-boy—three hundred and fifty dollars. She'd sell it if she could persuade the doctor to use the money to take a rest and travel— maybe to Paris, France. But the doctor takes a tour of the Civil War battlefields every two years and he says that's enough treat for anybody. Mrs. Gibbs will have to get around him somehow.

So the stage manager steers us around the village and it's afternoon before we know it and the children coming home from school. George Gibbs and Emily Webb walk together, making plans for a kind of telegraph between their two houses so that Emily may be able to give George a few hints about the Algebra problems. Arrived at her home, Emily pesters her mother with questions as they string beans together. "Am I pretty enough . . . to get anybody . . . to get people interested in me?" To which Mrs. Webb replies, "Emily, you make me tired. Now stop it. You're pretty enough for all normal purposes."

Evening comes. We hear the choir of the Congregational Church practice the hymns for the next church service under the direction of Simon Stimson who seems to have been drinking a little. After choir practice the women walk home and there is talk of the scandal that Simon's drinking is creating. Of course he's had lots of trouble—but a choir director and organist can't do that sort of thing. George Gibbs and Emily Webb are talking from their upper windows about Algebra—and the moon. So ends the day.

The next act is called Love and Marriage. Three years have gone by. The friendship of George and Emily has ripened into courtship. The stage manager pictures how it happened by placing a board across the backs of two chairs and two high stools behind it. It's a soda fountain and here are Emily and George sipping strawberry ice-cream sodas. The conversation began when George asked her if she were mad at him and she replied that she wasn't, but he's "got awful conceited and stuck-up" over his prowess in baseball. All the girls say so. George has taken this in the right spirit and invited her to have a soda and talk it over. His humility shames her and soon they are talking about how perfect men and women should be, and then what they are going to do when they graduate from high school. Before the sodas are finished George has made up his mind that he's not going to agricultural school. He thinks that "once you've found a person that you're very fond of . . . I mean a person who's fond of you, too,—at least enough to be interested in your character . . . Well, I think that's just as important as college is, and even more so."

Commencement has come and gone. The wedding follows. Yes, the parents have had to do a deal of adjusting to reconcile themselves to the idea of marriage for these youngsters, but they've been reasonably sensible about it and have come to the church to perform their parental parts. These are difficult. For first George, then Emily, suddenly struck with the importance and finality of the step they are taking and the break it will mean with their care-free life as adolescents, want to back out. George pleads with his mother that he doesn't want to be old, he just wants to be a "fella" . . . Emily begs of her father, "Why can't I stay for a while just as I am? . . . You used to say that I was *your* girl. Let's go away. I'll work for you. I could keep house." The parents calm the fears of the children and the marriage ceremony proceeds, the stage manager acting the minister's part.

Act Three is laid in the village cemetery nine years later and deals with the perspective of the dead upon the living. On the right-hand side of the stage, on ten or twelve ordinary chairs, sit the dead "in a quiet without stiffness, and in patience without listlessness." Mrs. Gibbs is here, and Wally Webb, and Simon Stimson and various others we met in earlier years. There is an empty chair for one whose funeral procession now winds toward this hillside—Emily Webb Gibbs who has died in the process of bearing her second child. The stage manager tells us the dead are waiting here while "the earth-part of 'em burns away . . . They're waitin' for something that they feel is comin' . . . Aren't they waitin' for the eternal part in them to come out clear?"

In a gentle rain, while the mourners attend to the last rites over Emily's grave, the dead talk quietly among themselves, not lugubriously but recollecting in tranquillity their days among the living. Then Emily comes to join them. Gradually, as she becomes accustomed to them, she tells Mrs. Gibbs of her life with George. They had made their farm a beautiful place, built a new barn and bought a great long cement drinking fountain for the stock. They bought that with the money Mrs. Gibbs had given them. Mrs. Gibbs doesn't remember the money, but we do. It was the three hundred and fifty dollars she got from her antique highboy; money which had not been used for that vacation tour.

By and by Emily learns that it is possible for her to return unseen among the living. The dead advise her not to do it: it will not be what she expects. But she insists on just one visit and she'll choose a happy day—her twelfth birthday, fourteen years ago. So she comes and we watch her re-living the events of that cold winter day—her father returning from Hamilton College, where he had made a speech, and bringing a birthday present for her; her mother warning her "birthday or no birthday, I want you to eat your breakfast. Chew that bacon slow. It'll help keep you warm on a cold day." Wally and her mother have presents for her, too, and there is a picture postcard from George. In the midst of it all she begs them to stop. "Oh, Mama, just look at me one minute as though you really saw me. Mama, fourteen years have gone by. I'm dead, I married George Gibbs. Wally's dead, too. . . . But just for a moment now we're all together. Mama, just for a moment we're happy. Let's look at one another." But the living are too busy. And when her father arrives, calling "Where's my girl? Where's my birthday girl?" she can stand it no longer and begs to be taken back—up the hill. But she bids them a last farewell. "Good-by, world. Good-by, Grover's Corners . . . Mama and Papa. Good-by to clocks ticking . . . and Mama's sunflowers. And food and coffee. And new-ironed dresses and hot baths . . . and sleeping and waking up. Oh, earth, you're too wonderful for anybody to realize you." And turning to the stage manager she asks through her tears, "Do any human beings ever realize life while they live it?—every, every minute?" And that philosopher answers, "No, the Saints and poets, maybe—they do some." Emily returns to the dead and they look at the stars and wait—wait "for the eternal part of them to come out clear."

Had this play ended with the second act it would doubtless have merited high rank among regional or *genre* dramas. Critics might have classified it as a New England play, or an idyl of small-town folk. Even so, the influence of Christ upon its major characters and upon the spiritual insights of the author would have been apparent. For the characters in their humanity transcend their Yankee locale and the author views their daily struggles with an understanding illumined by Christian compassion. But the third act, as John Gassner has said, "turns it into a classically poetic expression of the cycle of human existence from birth to death." Here the audience looks down from a place and time far above the earth and sees both living and dead in the light of the eternal stars. Human values and actions appear in their true proportions, and men and women as immortal souls of infinite significance. Little wonder then that the play was used widely in Europe as well as America during World War II or that the Italian people, although somewhat mystified by the first two acts, saw the third act as a companion-piece to Dante's *Divine Comedy*.

* * * * *

And so we conclude our study of the influence of Christ on the drama produced in the *theatres* of England and America. The reader may not have approved our selection of plays. He may have differed with our interpretation of the principal characters, the author's spiritual insight, and the total effect of this or that play. But he will surely agree that all these plays have two elements in common: they have sought sincerely to interpret life in terms of abiding spiritual values, and *we cannot imagine any of them written in a culture which Christ had not influenced.*

The theatres, however, have not housed all the drama of these two countries. During the last half-century a quietly growing but significant revival of drama in the *churches* has been under way. The story of that revival, and the influence of Christ upon it, will make the subject of our last chapter.

CHAPTER VI

Drama in the Modern Church

Two convictions underlie the modern revival of drama in the church. One is that Christianity's task is nothing less than the salvation of mankind—salvation *from* war and every other evil that destroys human beings; salvation *for* a coöperative world society of brotherhood. The other is that Christianity to be effective in the present age must be dramatized. The word "drama" is Greek and means "deeds" or "actions." To dramatize anything is to present it in terms of actions so that people may see it. Yet drama is more than visualization; it is an art with a structure of its own and shares with other arts the purpose of stirring and exalting the emotions. Our emotions are our springs of action. To dramatize Christianity, therefore, is to show it in action in such a way that the emotions—the springs of action—are exalted and directed to the salvation of man.

God, according to the Christian faith, has dramatized his love for man in countless ways, but supremely in the life of Christ. "The word became flesh and dwelt among us." That is still the world's greatest drama. Christ dramatized God's message in his teaching as well as in his life. The stories of the Prodigal Son and the Good Samaritan are typical examples of the way he portrayed religion in action and touched the hearts of men. To be sure, he had no physical stage; he used for his stage the imaginations of his hearers—"and the people heard him gladly." Even the most ignorant could understand a message so graphically told. With such a divine precedent for dramatizing religion the wonder is that the modern church has been slow in following it. Yet there were reasons.

In the theatre the influence of Christ has been hindered by the commercialism of men who exploit drama for private profit. Some of these are real estate speculators who control many of the playhouses and operate them for revenue only. Others are producers who speak of themselves as in "the show business," apparently unaware that historically this has been one of the last phases in the decline of drama. Among the exploiters, too, are those actors of the exhibitionist variety who use the drama as a ladder for their personal fame. In spite of such hindrances the influence of Christ has been unmistakable in the playwrights whose work we have discussed.

In the church one might hope that his influence would find no opposition in pervading the drama within its portals. It would be a vain and naïve hope. For while drama in the church has been practically free of commercialism it has had other devils to plague and torment it. Prejudice against the theatre dating back to the Puritans, low artistic standards, inexperienced directors, untrained actors, inadequate equipment, poor plays, worse productions, and confusion of purpose— these are a few of them. They have won many battles, but by no means all, and the struggle still goes on. To survey that struggle and the progress of the religious drama revival in America and England is our purpose in this chapter.

We have already seen that the modern drama began as a child of the Medieval church and grew up to be its prodigal son. In its childhood it was a means of making vivid the Bible to people who could not read it for themselves. We have seen, too, how the mystery and miracle plays of the Medieval church increased in popularity and, in time, moved from the church buildings to the churchyard, then to the marketplaces and street corners and courtyards of the inns. After the plays left the church they gradually lost their consciousness of a mission of salvation, became more and more permeated with folklore and comedy, and ultimately were completely secularized. They degenerated further until they fell under the censorship and ban of the Puritan reforms in England. So bitter was the church feeling against drama that centuries passed before religious leaders had either the inclination or the courage to revive it. But any prescient soul of the eighteenth century could have prophesied that the time would come when the church would put less emphasis on creed and more on understanding, and would return to its primary task of ministering to human beings in the midst of their daily conflicts. When that day came it would again call to its aid the art which has most to do with understanding and picturing those conflicts.

I. In America

No one can say just where and when that day came. Here and there in the eighteenth and nineteenth centuries individual churches in America made sporadic attempts to use drama as a means of communicating the Christian message. Nothing significant developed until about the beginning of the twentieth century and then only gradually. The remarkable feature of this modern revival of drama in the church and one that has determined much of its character since, was that it came into use not as an adult art but as an educational device for teaching children in Sunday Schools.

1. *Origin in Sunday Schools as an Educational Method*

Teachers and superintendents of these schools, dissatisfied with the traditional methods of printed lesson leaflets and cards bearing poorly colored scenes from Bible stories, began to experiment with visual demonstrations of various religious themes. Children dressed as angels with pasteboard wings of gold and glittering wire haloes trooped across Sunday School platforms heralding the coming of Christ. Or robed in more or less appropriate costumes, they re-enacted the scenes of the shepherds and the wise men, or proclaimed with childish naïveté God's call for Peace and Human Brotherhood. One could make a case for the indestructibility of the church on the ground that it survived some of these early Sunday School pageants. The amazing thing is that they drew crowds that filled the churches to overflowing when they were presented.

From this wobbly start the Sunday School teachers went on to the next phase—the informal acting out of stories of biblical characters. It was a natural step. A pageant centers around the visualization of an idea. A play centers round the portrayal of a character. Intelligent teachers who had discovered the popularity of ideas presented in pageant form began to ask themselves, Is our task with children and youth solely one of teaching them ideas, or is it to develop Christian *character*? There could be but one answer. No teacher worth his salt is content with instruction that is nothing more than the transmission of information and ideas to the mind of the student. He knows that beyond this function is the development of the whole personality of the student including his mind, his will, his affections. That is what drama is concerned with—not only with ideas, but with deeper springs of action in the emotions and the will. So the Sunday School teachers called drama to their aid and began to help the children re-live the great characters of the Bible. They dramatized the stories of Abraham and Isaac, David and Goliath, Joseph and his brethren, Ruth and Naomi, Elijah and the priests of Baal, and many more in Old Testament and New.

A personal illustration of this stage of the development of drama in the church may not be out of place. About twenty-five years ago the writer was confronted with a crisis in his own family. My two little boys—Richard six, and Arthur four years old—stood before me one evening as we were about to have our family altar. (It was our custom to read a passage from the Bible, have prayers, and then put the children to bed.) Said Richard, "We don't want any more of that stuff!"

"What's wrong with it?" I asked, astonished at this sudden rebellion.

"It's not interesting," he answered.

"What would you rather do?" I queried helplessly.

"We'd rather go to the movies." It did not seem to my wife and me that going to the movies was an adequate substitute for the family altar, although it had been done in some families. Suddenly an idea flashed across my mind.

"I think we can do something more interesting than the movies," I said. "Here in this old book are some stories we could act out ourselves. We could be the actors, the heroes, the villains, and all the rest. Wouldn't it be more fun than sitting and watching other fellows do the acting?"

They raised questions and I elaborated on the idea. Finally Richard asked, "Could we act out any story we want?"

"Of course," I agreed innocently. He made me promise this three times so that I was thoroughly committed. "What story would you like to do?"

"Adam and Eve," he announced triumphantly. Well, why not? It was not exactly the story we would have chosen, but we were a family of four with no audience to be shocked or pleased.

"All right, boys, Adam and Eve it shall be. What part do you want to play, Richard?"

"I want to be God, of course," he replied. At the age of six he usually wanted to be God all over the house, so that it was a piece of type-casting.

"And you, Arthur?"

"I want to be the serpent and crawl around on my tummy." That part seemed to fit his mischievous personality and it left my wife and me for the obvious parts of Eve and Adam. I told the boys that I would read the story just once and they had better listen carefully, for no one would tell them what to do if they forgot. They never listened as intently as they did that night. When I had finished I closed the book and turned to the young deity.

"Where will you have your Garden of Eden?"

"Here on the living room rug," he decided promptly. And then, beginning to feel his authority, he gave me a command. "Bring me that lamp!" I brought him a floor lamp. "It's a tree!" he declared. "Bring me that stool!" I brought it obediently. "It's a dog!" And so the work of creation went on until he had produced something representing to his mind a Garden of Eden.

Then came the supreme act—the creation of man. By this time his sense of power had become overwhelming. Turning upon me with fire in his eyes he fairly bellowed, "Lie down!" Now where in the world did that six-year-old get the idea that God bellows at his creatures? It's a mystery. At any rate I stretched myself on the rug and he knelt down beside me and went through the motions of heaping up clay and molding it into the shape of a man. As I peeked out from half-closed eyelids I detected a creative light in his face as if he thought he was making something out of nothing. Finally, when he had finished the job as well as he thought he could with such material he breathed his breath into my nostrils and whispered, "Adam!"—and I was created. He brought Eve into being in much the same way except that once he paused and came over and gave me a kick in the ribs to let me know that I had something to do with it. And so the story proceeded through the temptation by the irresistible four-year-old serpent, the indictment of the guilty pair by their offended Creator, and on down to the last scene where in the Bible story God shows his compassion for Adam and Eve by providing them with clothes so they will not be cold when they leave the garden. But Richard forgot this tender touch. Leading us to the edge of the rug he gave us a violent shove as he shouted, "Out you go!"

We had so much fun that first night that we went on to do other stories in the weeks and months that followed. My wife and I were delighted to see that the boys did not think of them as scientific accounts of the creation or as history. They treated them simply as imaginative stories. Their own imaginations kindled as they acted them out and they came quickly to appreciate what it means to look at the world through the eyes of others, and to feel as others feel. That is the underlying principle of good acting; it is also the basis of the Golden Rule. I think that they came to understand also something of the effect of internal attitudes upon outer actions and upon character.

Multiply this example by hundreds, even thousands, and we have a rough idea of why and how churches came to use "creative dramatics" in developing the characters of their young people and in teaching them the Bible stories and other tales of lasting worth. Several books have recorded the experience of individual churches and teachers employing this method. Among them two of the most useful are Elizabeth Erwin Miller's *Dramatization of Bible Stories* and Hulda Niebuhr's *Ventures in Dramatics*.

2. *From Children's Plays to Adult Bible Dramas*

The next step was the introduction of formal dramas prepared by playwrights using at least the basic principles of dramaturgy and requiring for actors more mature young people and adults. The Bible still furnished the characters and the themes of these plays. They were mostly one-act dramas, for these fitted best the capacities of the players and the one-hour limit of most Sunday evening church services. These plays marked the beginning of what we may call audience-focus; that is, they were designed not primarily as a classroom technique for educating the players but as a means of inspiring the congregation. Director and cast and crew put in dozens of hours of rehearsal, scene-building, staging, and costuming and then presented their play to a congregation of adults and youth as a part of the regular Sunday evening worship service.

The service usually began in the traditional manner with hymns, scripture, prayer, responses—all appropriate to the biblical theme of the play. Then, in place of the usual sermon, came the drama. At its conclusion a hymn and the benediction brought the service to a close. When the play was well written and produced the congregation experienced that lift of spirit that religion speaking through art always creates.

One of the plays of this type that proved most effective was

Charles Rann Kennedy's "The Terrible Meek," a tense story of a Roman officer's struggle with his conscience after the crucifixion of Jesus. Written in poetic prose, its three characters— the captain, a soldier, and Mary the mother of Jesus—unfolded the story in almost total darkness in a setting representing the barren hill-top at the foot of the cross. Although it had no biblical basis except the fact of the crucifixion, it epitomized in the Roman officer the conflict of all sensitive souls of every age: the conflict between loyalty to a temporal empire built on force and loyalty to Christ's kingdom built on love.

Another biblical drama in one act was Mary Hamlin's "He Came Seeing." Taking as its theme the price one must be ready to pay for being a follower of Christ, it built a poignant tale around the blind beggar boy healed by the Master and later brought under coercion by the Pharisees to make him deny his Lord. Both Mr. Kennedy and Mrs. Hamlin used modern, rather than archaic, English in their plays and brought out the timeless human traits of their characters so effectively that these dramas are still widely used. A dozen or more similar one-act dramas furnished dramatic material for the church as it attempted to make vividly real to adult congregations the eternal truths in the Bible. And some of them continue to serve this fundamental need of the modern church.

3. *From Biblical to Modern Dramas and a New Definition of Religious Drama*

About 1925 a new demand arose. Young people began to ask, "Why must we act out only the struggles of men and women who lived two thousand years ago? Don't people today have battles just as important? Isn't our religion interested in them?" Out of the answers to such questions came the development of modern religious drama in the church. In the earlier days it had been thought that a drama was religious only when it drew its story and characters from the Bible; or when the people in the plays or pageants talked much about Christ and the church. Inevitably, though, we have come to see that what makes a play religious is *not its subject matter* but its *total effect* upon an audience. This has led to a new definition of religious drama. Today we define it as *any drama which has a religious effect; that is, it sends an audience away exalted in mood and with a deepened sense of fellowship with God and man*. Thus a play may deal with any subject matter that is human—work, play, love, worship—it may have as its locale any place on the earth or in the sky; it may be peopled with sinners of any and every class, color, creed and hair-do. If the author has so treated his material, his subject, and his characters that he has created a strong drama and the total effect of that drama is religious, then he has written a religious drama. Some of these plays are biblical; but an increasing number picture the spiritual struggles, individual and social, of our own times. They seek to present them honestly and courageously and with the spiritual insights of Christ.

4. *Creating New and Better Plays*

This development has not come in a day or a year, or without growing pains. Obviously plays of this sort require more maturity in thought and skill in craftsmanship than adaptations of biblical material where situation and characters are already created. The church thus far has not made any serious attempt to train such playwrights. Nor has it found a way to provide any adequate compensation for the time and labor of skilled dramatists and directors. It usually takes a competent playwright at least a month to create a one-act play of merit, and at least three months for a full-length drama. Few writers have independent incomes sufficient to enable them to volunteer this time. In the professional theatre they can afford to gamble in the hope that if their plays are produced they will be guaranteed a minimum compensation and a percentage of the box-office returns. In the church there are no box-office returns. The only compensation the author receives is from the publisher. This, for a one-act play, usually varies from $15 to $50 if published royalty-free. If a royalty of $5 per presentation is charged (few churches ever pay more and most prefer to pay nothing) the author customarily receives half of this. Thus a play will have to be presented a hundred times before the author receives $250 for his month's labor on a one-act play, and three hundred times before he receives $750 for his three months' work on a full-length play. This system is not satisfactory either to churches or competent authors. It is probably the basic reason why so few professional dramatists create dramas for the church.

Back of this lies the failure of religious leaders to appreciate the potentiality of the art to minister to the souls of men. Too many have looked upon drama in the church only as a "new wrinkle" in religious education, a passing fad, something to keep young people occupied, or a happy outlet for the creative energies of the minister's wife. Others have viewed it as a comparatively painless way to inform their congregations concerning the financial needs of the church and its mission boards and similar agencies.

The net result of these two factors—the failure to provide

compensation for authors and the failure to appreciate the potentiality of drama as a medium of ministry—was to slow down the development of modern drama that combined artistic strength and religious power. Church agencies and commercial publishers issued a flood of propaganda pageants and playlets at low prices and these constituted the bulk of the first dramatic fare that was not biblical. Most of this material was written by well-meaning persons who wanted to help a particular cause—missions, stewardship, peace, etc.—but had never taken the trouble to study the basic principles of dramaturgy. Here and there a good modern play appeared, but most of the so-called religious dramas of the decade before 1925 were a saccharine and sticky mess of sentimentality permeated with propaganda or with pious sermonizing.

Such a situation might well have been the death of a movement less imbued with the vigor of youth and a sense of high and unselfish purpose. As it was, instead of succumbing to discouragement, the more sophisticated young drama groups began to refuse to produce this material. They demanded real plays—plays that had reality of characterization, skill in construction, and relevance to daily life. This demand became so strong that in 1924 the Federal Council of Churches appointed a committee to survey the available supply of religious plays and to select a few that could be recommended.

The writer was chairman of that committee. We read hundreds of the dramas then being offered and finally chose ten that we thought worthy. Among these were Kenneth Sawyer Goodman's "Dust of the Road" (a story of a modern man tempted to betray a trust), four or five of the better biblical plays mentioned above, Percy MacKaye's "The Pilgrim and the Book," Elisabeth Woodbridge's "The Crusade of the

Children," and two or three others. The volume—*Religious Dramas, 1924,* now out of print—met with a grateful response from church drama groups, for the plays marked a distinct advance in quality of dramatic writing. Yet their subject matter was primarily biblical or concerned with other bygone days. With the exception of Goodman's play none attempted to picture modern spiritual struggles. Up to that time no modern one-act plays of this kind had been published—at least none had reached the attention of our editorial committee.

Four years later, however, I was able to compile a volume of short plays nearly all of which centered about contemporary conflict situations interpreted with spiritual insight. Among the dramas of this volume [1] were Zona Gale's "Neighbors," a humorous portrayal of some very human village folk who rally to the relief of a needy neighbor; Percival Wilde's "Confessional," a capsule tragedy of a man whose reputation for integrity has no inner roots; Virginia Church's "What Men Live By," a dramatization of the famous story by Tolstoi; Hall and Middlemass' "The Valiant," a sombre but moving play about a criminal trying to keep the knowledge of his shame from his family; Fred Eastman's "Bread," dealing with the struggle of a farm family for culture as well as bread; J. M. S. Tompkins' "The Deathless World," a fantasy of the future when science will have discovered how to prolong life indefinitely, but not how to make it worth living; Irene Taylor MacNair's "The Color Line," picturing the conflicts, internal and external, of an Oriental Christian student on an American college campus; and W. R. Bowie's "Christmas Pageant of the Holy Grail." The timeliness of such plays, combined with

---

[1] *Modern Religious Dramas,* Henry Holt and Co., 1928; revised edition, Harper and Bros, 1938; second revision, Walter H. Baker Co., 1947.

their artistic quality (far from perfect) and their religious effect gave them wide appeal. This volume has gone through three editions and several printings.

Since then several other compilations of religious dramas have appeared, notably Charles Rann Kennedy's *Plays for Seven Players*, Harold Ehrensperger's *Plays to Live By*, Dorothy Clarke Wilson's *Twelve Months of Drama*, Isabel Kimball Whiting's *Dramatic Preludes and Services of Worship*, and the present writer's *Ten One-Act Plays*. Serious workers in the field of religious drama now had, by 1933, at least a small library of selected plays.

5. *Raising Standards of Production*

But the old quip that you can lead a boy to college but you can't make him think still proved true. It was not enough that the church should have a library of religious plays of tested merit. Their value must be demonstrated in action and before audiences. Yet they could not be so demonstrated on a wide scale without good productions. That meant that drama directors and players must be trained in the rudiments of directing, acting, staging, rehearsing, costuming, lighting, etc. Some of this a few had received in high schools and colleges; these formed the nuclei of training groups. Other amateur actors in church dramas displayed the same resistance to disciplined training that so many college students manifest toward the acquisition of knowledge. To help them through these growing pains various church organizations now began experimental efforts, some local, some regional, and some national. Typical examples of these endeavors to improve the quality of productions are the following:

The Methodist, Presbyterian, Episcopal, Baptist, Congregational, and other denominations through their national departments of religious education or similar agencies, added short courses in drama production to their regular summer conference programs. These courses were short indeed, lasting usually only ten days to three weeks, but they provided elementary training in acting and in production methods, and they stimulated the imaginations of the young people to see what they could do and their wills to accomplish it. During the next few years literally thousands received such stimulus.

In 1924, after three years of thinking and talking about it, Methodist college students founded the National Society of Wesley Players with its first chapters in the University of Illinois, Iowa State College, the University of Wisconsin, and Ohio State University. By 1942 it had added twenty-six more chapters in as many colleges and universities between the Atlantic and the Pacific. This national society has worked consistently for higher standards of production, conducted play-writing contests, held regional and national conferences, and published a magazine, *The Footlight,* an organ of fellowship and exchange of experience in religious drama production.

Several church federations, as in Cleveland, Chicago, and Baltimore, set up annual religious drama tournaments to improve by competition the quality of acting and directing. The Ohio Council of Churches developed a state-wide tournament of this nature. The Religious Drama Council of the Greater New York Federation of Churches came into being "to discover all interests, talents and resources in the domain of Religious Drama and, through mutual inspiration and coöperative action, to encourage the use of Religious Dramaturgy in the programs of our churches and church schools." In fulfillment of this purpose it has issued selected lists of plays, conducted playwriting contests, and held festivals of religious dramas.

Individual churches—at least a few of the larger ones—employed drama directors on full or part time to utilize the latent talent in their congregations and in the surrounding community in programs of drama for educational and worship services. The Riverside Church in New York inaugurated such a plan under the direction of Mr. and Mrs. Omar Goslin. The record of its major achievements in worship programs made a sizable and valuable volume entitled *Worship Through Drama.* The Madison Avenue Presbyterian Church (New York) specialized in educational uses of creative dramatics of a religious nature under the direction of Miss Hulda Niebuhr. Her excellent book, *Ventures in Dramatics,* was one by-product. In Los Angeles the amazingly vigorous First Congregational Church established a Religious Drama Workshop under the able direction of Miss Nelle C. Wiley. This workshop ran the year around with evening classes in playwriting, directing, staging, costuming, and lighting, enrolling more than a hundred students. By the coöperative work of these classes this church produced three long and eight or more short plays each year with an expertness seldom attained in church drama. In Grand Rapids, at the Fountain Street Baptist Church, Miss Amy Loomis for many years has demonstrated the effectiveness of drama when plays and pageants are well selected and presented by disciplined actors working with adequate equipment.

The churches of many smaller cities and rural communities pooled their resources to form drama circuits. For example, in Portland, Maine, in 1931 four churches organized such a circuit that worked after this manner: the players of each church prepared a different play, produced it first in their own church and then took it on succeeding Sunday evenings to the three other churches. Thus each group had the advantage of presenting its play to four congregations, thereby justifying the long hours of the original preparation, and learning something from the demands made upon their adaptability as they worked with the vai ing equipment of the respective congregations. The congregations, in turn, had four dramatic services where otherwise they would have had but one. Rev. Ralph Stoody, one of the originators of this plan, wrote concerning its effect on the players: "They feel a deep sense of reward for their effort when they know that they are preparing not for one thirty-minute presentation but for four appearances before four different audiences. They are willing to attempt somewhat more difficult vehicles . . . Knowing that their own production will be compared by each congregation with the others, there is an added stimulus to good work."

The Roman Catholic Church has worked independently and its dramatic activities have been in keeping with its size and its doctrine. Emmet Lavery, author of *The First Legion, Monsignor's Hour* and the stage version of *Yankee from Olympus* and many other plays, has been outstanding among the Catholic leaders in drama. He estimates that some five thousand school, college, parish and community units among the Catholics produce religious plays annually or more often. Among its best-known larger units are the Loyola Theatre of Chicago, the Catholic Repertory Theatre at Our Lady of Lourdes Church in New York City, and Mundelein and Rosary Colleges in Chicago. The National Catholic Theatre Conference, founded in 1937, acts as a clearing-house for the many dramatic organizations among the Catholics and seeks to advance the quality of their work. Mr. Lavery, a member of its executive committee, says that it "is trying to get more groups to do more of the better plays the same year, and to get colleges to make room for at least one new play each year." The Conference has its headquarters at the Catholic University in Washington, D. C.

The Church of the Latter Day Saints (Mormon), also working independently, has developed higher standards through a unique plan. It conducts its drama work through its Young Men's and Young Women's Mutual Improvement Society which has "Amusement Halls" in two thousand centers of the United States and Canada, each hall equipped with a little theatre where from three to six plays are presented every year. To provide these groups with selected plays of quality the central organization purchases from various publishers both the re-print and production rights of six or more plays of the royalty class and publishes them in a volume which it sells to its local units at $2.50. The local unit is thus relieved of royalty obligations. It is not required to use the plays from the volume, but it would have to look far and pay more to secure better plays. Directors are carefully selected, too, and made responsible to a trained dramatic supervisor. Brigham Young University through its Speech Department serves as clearing house for information and exchange of experience. A monthly magazine, *Era,* publishes news of drama developments throughout the world. And each year the church holds a Drama Festival at Salt Lake City where seeded dramatic units with honor casts present their plays to large audiences.

The Chicago Theological Seminary, recognizing the importance of drama not only as a means of communicating the

Christian faith but as a dynamic instrument for cultivating
the imagination of students for the ministry, established a
chair in Religious Literature and Drama in 1926 and has
maintained it ever since. It offers four courses in drama. The
first is a survey in which the student reads and analyzes the
great religious dramas of the centuries, from the days of
ancient Greece to the present. The second is a study of the
works of such spiritually sensitive playwrights of the modern
theatre as we have discussed in the earlier chapters of this
book. The third is a workshop in production where the student seeks to present plays with a minimum of mechanical
equipment and a maximum of religious effect. The fourth is
a course in playwriting. All these courses are electives. After
twenty years of observation of their results it is not too much
to say that the students who have elected them have developed
a deeper appreciation of the dramas of daily life. They have
become more imaginative preachers. Often they have revealed
more of that understanding that marks the difference between
a dry parson and a man of spiritual power.

Such, in brief, have been the main phases in the development of drama in the modern church in America, and such
a few of the efforts to improve its standards of playwriting and
spontaneous attempt to meet a need. It has received no organized promotion or publicity outside of a few denomina-
tional offices. Only a few articles about it have appeared in
drama magazines and few, if any, in the secular press. To
this day it is probably unknown to the dramatic critics of
Broadway; which is a pity, for the workers in religious drama
would have profited by their constructive criticism. Yet its
extent, if not its artistic quality, amazes one who studies the
facts concerning it.

6. *Present State of Religious Drama in American Churches*

A bird's eye view of this extent and of the state of religious drama in this country in the year 1940 may be glimpsed from a summary of a survey made at the end of that year by The Chicago Theological Seminary. The survey included 364 churches, each with a membership of 300 or more, selected as samples from six denominations and located in nine geographical areas. The denominations included Methodist, Congregational Christian, Disciples, Northern Baptist, Presbyterian, and Episcopal. The geographical areas were New England, Middle Atlantic, South Atlantic, Northeast Central, Southeast Central, Northwest Central, Southwest Central, Mountain and Pacific.

Of the 364 churches reporting, 322, or almost 90 per cent, declared that they were producing plays as a part of their regular program. They had presented 876 in 1940—an average of 2.7 plays per church. What reason did they assign for producing these plays? More than half replied that their purpose was "the inspiration of the audience." About a third checked "for the education of the players." (Some, of course, checked both.) Less than a fifth said that they used the plays "to raise money." Only a few indicated that their plays were of a non-religious variety "for entertainment."

What types of plays were these churches using? Their answers disclosed that 36 per cent were biblical, 49 per cent non-biblical but religious, 15 per cent non-religious.

What groups produced the plays, and on what occasions? Mixed groups of adults and young people presented about 60 per cent, young people about 25 per cent, and children 10 per cent. More than 55 per cent of the plays were presented during the Christmas season, about 20 per cent around Easter, the rest at various times throughout the year. Usually the churches presented their plays at the Sunday evening service, but about one-fourth of the total were given on midweek "church nights."

A few of the handicaps under which the drama groups of these churches labored are revealed in the cold statistics they report concerning their equipment—or lack of it. Only one church in three had a permanent stage with a proscenium arch. About one in five had some sort of temporary stage. The rest—nearly half—had nothing but a platform. For lighting, the churches seem to have relied mostly upon makeshift arrangements. Of the 322 churches, 170 had spotlights, 161 had floodlights, 173 had footlights (the least necessary), and only 84 had borderlights, although the latter are perhaps the most useful of the various lighting units for drama.

If the survey had ended here it might have left the impression that modern religious drama had come safely through its growing pains and was moving along rather smartly except for its material equipment. But it did not stop there. The surveyors (students specializing in religious drama at The Chicago Theological Seminary) were concerned with getting the facts about quality as well as quantity. To what extent had the church drama groups freed themselves from the blight of plays weak in dramatic quality and permeated with propaganda and sentimentality? To arrive at some estimate of this they asked for the titles of the plays produced in 1940, then checked these titles against those included in the compilations of better plays mentioned above and against the much larger lists of recommended plays issued by various inter-denominational committees. Most of the plays used by the churches were not on the recommended lists. Instead, they "consisted largely of cheap, non-royalty plays which would hardly be accepted by any but a generous church congregation whose own members were participants."

The report of the survey concluded:

No honest interpretation of the findings . . . can ignore their dark side. In spite of the constructive examples cited the bulk of the religious drama in this country seems still on the level of mediocrity. Its religious effectiveness suffers accordingly. The reasons for this mediocrity lie in poor selection of plays, inadequate discipline of directors and players, wretched equipment, low standards of dramatic art, and confused thinking about the purpose of drama in the church.

The average dramatic group wants "to put on a play." Too often the director, whose only experience has been the production of high school plays, has at hand no selected list of good plays. He (or she) simply asks the group, "Does anyone know of a play he'd like us to do?" Or he thumbs through a publisher's catalog looking for plays of the right length and cast-size and requiring no royalty. Less than a tenth of the plays produced by the churches studied could pass the tests of good dramaturgy.

The churches which have had the best success in play production have found that only first-class plays have the quality necessary to reward their players or . . . the audience . . . They have found, too, that the first-class plays are cheaper in the long run, for they build up audiences and the free-will offerings are correspondingly increased. The larger and more enthusiastic the audience, the better the players respond. In time, with careful business management, the group can buy more adequate equipment, wardrobe and library. It will have, too, the support and constructive criticism of the more intelligent people of the community without which artistic standards languish.

The dark side of the picture will quickly disappear and drama in the churches take on new dignity and effectiveness when the ministers, the directors and the players realize the tremendous power available in this art to minister to the human soul. Suppose a church drama group, instead of thinking of "putting on a play," thinks of dramatizing religion in action. It will have set its head and heart in the right direction. It will then choose plays that present human beings who have struggled through great spiritual conflicts such as we now face. These plays will not be propaganda plays for boards and agencies, or pseudo-dramatic appeals to raise the church budget. They will be strong dramas of the spirit. Some of them will center around the prophets and saints of the centuries past. Others will portray the heroic strivings of men and women of our own day. They will be plays that lift the audience and stir its noblest emotions . . .

A dramatic group that has such a purpose will demand—and get—the equipment it needs. It will seek the severest discipline. It will think of itself as in the great succession of the players of the Greek tragedies and the medieval mysteries. Its task and opportunity are as great as theirs.[2]

When the church heeds that call the influence of Christ through its drama will grow in strength and in power to bless human life. For even under its present handicaps and restrictions, drama in the modern church has demonstrated that it is not simply a new wrinkle in religious education. It is no fad. Its roots go down to the beginnings of religion. Its modern warrant lies in the need of our troubled times for a spiritual ministry to millions of worried and confused men and women. Those dramatists and directors who understand the potentialities of their art are using it to develop strength, beauty and

[2] Quotation and preceding data are from the author's article "Present State of Religious Drama" in *The Christian Century*, February 26, 1941.

power in the inner life of players and congregations. They have discovered in their own experience that drama at its best can kindle the imaginations, purge and exalt the emotions, interpret life in language of the heart, and challenge the will to action. The fruit of their efforts so used is in human lives enriched in understanding, sympathy and fellowship.

II. IN ENGLAND

Drama in the church in modern England began about the same time as in America; that is, shortly after the turn of the present century. Also as in America, it originated in local churches as an instrument for teaching children and youth the stories of the Bible. Doubtless the vigorous growth of amateur drama of a secular nature in schools and communities further influenced it. But it remained in local parishes and experimental until the 1920's. Then, strangely enough, it received a strong impetus from the great explorer, Sir Francis Younghusband, whose explorations in Asia had brought him in contact with the striking use the communists there were making of drama in spreading their gospel among the masses. When he returned to England he became a prime mover in the organization of the Religious Drama Council of England, Scotland and Wales (now the Religious Drama Society), for he was convinced that Christians should be at least as energetic in promoting their religion as the communists were in theirs. Mr. Laurence Housman, one of England's ablest poets and dramatists, became the first head of this Council and his charming series of short plays entitled *Little Plays of St. Francis* greatly aided the movement.

1. *Parish Development of Religious Drama*

Since then it has flowed in two streams, one parochial, the other national, but both with the aid and blessing of the Religious Drama Society. The parochial has followed a course remarkably parallel to that in America, local churches working independently and with similar handicaps: inadequate resources in money and equipment, poor plays, untrained actors, inexperienced directors, confusion of purpose. Nevertheless it has spread over the country until most churches have at least an annual medieval nativity play, and some a passion play and scenes from the lives of saints and modern missionaries. At first, the artistic quality of most of these hardly compared with that of secular drama groups. As in America the church seemed to specialize on "cheap and easy" productions with correspondingly poor results. This was the situation when the Religious Drama Society took hold. It has sought to raise the standards—and the resulting effectiveness—of these parish plays by issuing selected lists of better plays, making available a library for directors, holding conferences and schools for drama leaders, publishing bulletins and manuals, and by clarifying the purpose of drama in the church. On the latter point, Mr. E. Martin Browne, a director of the Society, writes: "We need to re-establish in the minds of all who have to do with it that *drama is not an exposition but an experience*: that the play exists to enable actors and audience together to become part of the divine essence for a revealing moment." [3]

To break the pattern of medieval plays, on the revival of which the parish churches seemed concentrating some twenty

[3] This and subsequent quotations from Mr. Browne are from his article in *The Christian News-Letter* (London) and are used by permission.

years ago, Mr. Housman and Rev. H. R. L. Sheppard (also a poet and one of the most dynamic of the younger religious leaders) made a bold experiment. They produced a Christmas play in which they presented the holy family in modern costumes with Joseph as a Welsh miner out of work. But the shock was too great to receive either critical or popular approval for their effort. They persisted nevertheless, and gradually plays of contemporary life began to come into use. In 1928 Mr. Housman challenged the church drama groups further in an address reported in the *London Times* as follows:

If you are to have live drama [said Laurence Housman], it must touch modern problems and conditions, even somewhat controversially perhaps. If the churches are to be alive they must show fight. If they dare not have drama that shows fight they are not going to have live drama, and the subject is closed. The question is: How can you set up live drama which will also be religious drama?

The real problem you are up against is a moral, a spiritual, problem. Is Christ still the Great Adventurer or is he only a reminiscence? Is to be Christian still the greatest social problem of today, or is it only a tradition? Are you going to put into your religious drama only those versions of Christianity which fit into our system, which Caesar accepts and can make use of; or are you prepared to give Caesar the lie and to give institutional Christianity the lie when they bear false witness against what Christianity should stand for? On your answer to these questions depends whether or not you can have live drama in your churches.

If you mean to have live drama you must have the courage of your convictions and be ready to do the unfamiliar and unexpected thing. Put to yourselves this as a test: You are willing to have in your churches a mystery play, or something similar, from past ages; but are you equally willing to have a modern play, not merely a goody-goody play of pious, blameless characters, but a play of social conflict, like "Strife," or a play exposing legal cruelty, like "Justice," by Galsworthy? I do not mean necessarily those plays in particular, but plays generally as socially alive to our own times. Are you willing, incidentally, to have laughter? I think you must have it if your religious drama is to be free and worth while. In fact, not to be shocked at good laughter is one of the reforms in church convention most needed today.

If you ask me how to come by religious drama, take anything in the present social system you believe to be wrong and unchristian, tackle it ruthlessly and uncompromisingly, as you think it ought to be tackled. Show it up, make it as modern as you like, as controversial as you like; and if you have the dramatic gift and if your solution is a Christian solution, you have religious drama. You ask me for subjects? War, capital punishment, the soul-destroying system of our prisons, sweated labor, prostitution, the hardness of heart of the self-righteous, the color problem—out of all these you can get religious drama.

And out of all those the more alert dramatists came more and more to fashion their plays.

2. *National Development of Religious Drama*

But the unique and major stream of the movement, and the one which has most successfully engaged the attention of the Society, is the national one. Its goal is nothing less than the production of religious dramas of the highest quality presented in England's most hallowed shrines before great congregations. Leadership for this broad-visioned project was furnished by the Dean of Canterbury who presented in that historic cathedral at Whitsuntide in 1928 the premier production of Masefield's *Coming of Christ* (described in Chapter IV). A year later, on becoming the Bishop of Chichester, he appointed a director of religious drama for his diocese. This director's duties included the management of a travelling company to demonstrate in local parishes the value of drama in education and in spiritual ministry. It was largely due to the Bishop of Chichester that Canterbury Cathedral inaugurated in the following year the annual Festival of the Arts which has since become world famous. For this Festival a group known as "Friends of Canterbury Cathedral" enlisted the services of distinguished poets and playwrights beginning with T. S. Eliot, who wrote for it *Murder in the Cathedral,* which proved so successful that it was soon being produced in leading theatres in America as well as England. Other plays which received their first productions at Canterbury included Charles Williams' *Cranmer,* Christopher Hassall's *Christ's Comet* and Dorothy Sayers' *The Zeal of Thy House* and *The Devil to Pay.* The mounting popularity of the dramatic productions of this Festival prompted Tewkesbury and other cathedrals to undertake similar projects—all of them interrupted, however, by the outbreak of the war in 1939.

3. *The Pilgrim Players*

But the war did not stop the religious drama movement; it only changed its immediate nature and application. Within a few months the Religious Drama Society, with the collaboration of several of the leading clergymen and such well-known actors as John Gielgud, Dame Sybil Thorndike and Dame Marie Tempest, sponsored a new group of professional actors called "The Pilgrim Players" to minister through drama to civilians and soldiers in the thick of a war that threatened the extinction of their country and themselves. Mr. E. Martin

Browne, who later became their director, wrote in 1942 concerning them:

They have toured Britain from the Orkneys to Penzance and in well over two thousand performances have given plays almost exclusively religious to every variety of audience, service and civilian, young and old, ecclesiastical and secular. Their adventures would make a book by themselves. . . . The quality and wide dissemination of their work have made the drama of religion acceptable to the people of this island as never before.

Two years after The Pilgrim Players began their touring, some letters from their first director, Miss Ruth Spalding, to her mother, Mrs. H. N. Spalding of Lenox, Massachusetts, came into my hands. Mrs. Spalding has kindly allowed me to use them. They are among the most remarkable and courageous letters I have ever read. They describe a project carried on under circumstances probably not equaled since the early Christians defied a Roman dictator's ban and met for worship in the catacombs. Here is a typical scene as I reconstruct it from the information in one of Miss Spalding's letters:

Incendiary bombs were falling on London. The center of the ancient city was ablaze. Cultural landmarks, centuries old, were going up in smoke. Detonations of Hitler's heavier hell-openers shook the earth. But down underneath the ruins of a church, in its crypt, some hundreds of men, women, and children were witnessing a group of actors presenting a religious drama. Should the play stop? the director asked of the motley audience. "No, no! Carry on, please!" came the answer. And the play went on. "It was grand to have something to give them," wrote Miss Spalding. "They were as silent and responsive an audience as we have ever experienced."

They played in all sorts of buildings ranging from garages, barns, and village schools to Blenheim Palace and Salisbury Cathedral. They numbered but five men and three women. Their weekly expenses (including a minimum guaranteed salary of seven dollars a week for each actor) amounted to about $180. This low figure permitted them to give their plays for a "top" of sixty cents admission, or even to dispense with ticket sales and depend on free-will offerings. Their repertory consisted at first of four full-length plays—*The Holly and the Ivy*, a Christmas comedy by Noel Martin; *Twelve Thousand*, by Bruno Frank; *Tobias and the Angel*, by James Bridie (their most popular piece, founded on the Apocryphal Book of Tobit); and *The Terror of Light*, a verse play about Pentecost by Charles Williams—and half a dozen short dramas.

Extracts from her letters: "We have discovered that we can play the strongest religious plays to the troops! A public relations officer, a hard-headed man, told us that we ought to play to them real religious plays like *The Way of the Cross*. So we gave it, and they were about the grandest audience we ever played to. They simply loved it. The cast feels that this is one of the most worth-while things we can do. Through it came many other invitations to play to military and R.A.F. camps round about." . . . Some days later: "The response to our work lately has been terrifically cheering. There is so much work to do that we wonder whether soon we ought not have a puppy company, as we cannot meet the demand." The second company was soon formed. "The demand increases all the time. . . . I think our heads might be turned only that it is very clear that all the glorious things that happen to us can't really be our doing or our deserts, but are the gifts of the Holy Spirit, which blesses our poor little loaves and fishes." From London, where they arrived just in time to experience the great fire-blitz: "We played in East End air raid shelters, in a Barking Baptist Mission shelter, in a shelter in Quixley Street, East India Dock (where we played at the end of a grubby passage, with small urchins pushing on to the 'stage' from all sides, and then to an audience seated on different tiers of their bunks).... We played also in the crypt of St. Paul's—the first play St. Paul's has ever countenanced." And finally, this from the last of her letters that I had the privilege to read: "There are relatively few theatrical companies that have survived till now, so we have the exciting and responsible position of being among the few in charge of the modern theatre and, in a humble way, in charge of a new tradition that is, perforce, coming in: improvisation, simplicity; plays of significance instead of dead drawing-room comedies; actors who act because they love the job, not for the reward or the limelight."

A movement vital enough to adapt itself to the desperate need of the English people in wartime, and with such inspiring effect, has proved its worth on the level of human survival. It will endure when all the escape-from-life dramas are blown away in the storms that sweep across this troubled world.

When the war ended, the Pilgrim Players decided to continue their ministry, for the need of it had not passed. They opened their peacetime program in September, 1945, at the Mercury Hill Theatre of London with a dramatization of the story of Elijah in the setting of modern Cumberland—*The Old Man of the Mountains* by Norman Nicholson. They followed it with a masque, *This Way to the Tomb,* by Robert Duncan with music by Benjamin Ritter. At this writing they are carrying on.

4. *Radio Drama: "The Man Born to Be King"*

One other venture of great significance in religious drama as well as in radio belongs in this record. Early in 1940 the Director of Religious Broadcasting for the British Broadcasting Company invited Miss Dorothy Sayers, widely known for her religious dramas as well as for her detective stories, to write a cycle of radio plays on the Life of Our Lord. She accepted and worked upon the series during 1940 and 1941—as difficult an assignment as any writer could undertake, given the rigid time and technical requirements of radio and the immense amount of scholarly research necessary to get the facts straight and to present them accurately in condensed form, not to mention the innumerable problems of interpretation. One can readily believe her statement when she handed in the last script that she had "worn out one Greek Testament and amassed a considerable theological library."

Ten days before the first play of the cycle was to be broadcast it was announced at a Press Conference. While most of the reporters wrote fairly and sympathetically about it, a few treated it sensationally and inaccurately, terming the whole project "irreverent," "blasphemous," and "vulgar." These reports stirred up a storm of protest so violent that the propriety of the venture was questioned in the House of Commons and the BBC had to postpone the second program for a fortnight "to allow a fuller consideration of the plays at a meeting of the Religious Advisory Committee." Fortunately this seems to have been an unusual advisory committee, for its members—all high-ranking churchmen of various denominations—had all read the plays. Unanimously, in spite of the disapproving clamor from angry laymen, they pledged their public sup-

port of the plays. Thereupon the BBC went on with the
series.

The twelve programs in this cycle, entitled "The Man Born
to Be King," were presented once each month during the year
1942 and again in shorter intervals in 1943, and will probably
be repeated often in years to come. For they turned out to be
one of the most popular features ever broadcast by the BBC,
reaching two million listeners. Not all of these, by any means,
reacted favorably. Many, instead of exercising their right not
to listen, organized opposition designed to prevent others from
doing so. Some went so far as to blame these plays for the fall
of Singapore and urged that they be stopped before a similar
fate befall Australia! But the Lord seems to have a way of
"making the wrath of man to please him," and it may have
been that the wide hearing they received resulted in part from
this advertising. Yet the BBC wisely declined to accept the
thanks offered by one grateful listener who opined that the
plays "made possible the November victories in Libya and
Russia." All crank-mail aside, however, the BBC has on file a
large sheaf of letters of profound gratitude for this series. Here
is a typical one:

Your play, *The Man Born to Be King,* is quite changing the
atmosphere in our house, and where there has been resentment
and criticism, we can feel it all dying away in the presence of
Christ. I am sure this must be the case in all homes where they
have heard it broadcast.

Thus the influence of Christ has reached through the airways
into the homes of England.

The future of religious drama in England? No one has
written more thoughtfully and confidently in answer to that

question than Mr. Browne: "The scope is huge. The chance is unique. The moment is now. For the religious drama is fuller of life at this moment than ever before. It has won the respect of the theatre as well as of the church. There is still plenty of prejudice to overcome . . . but it is possible that the national and civic theatres, which are coming at long last to this country, may reckon religion among the themes with which their plays should deal. The churches should support with all their might the formation of such theatres. . . . The church and the stage can thus come together again for the benefit of both."

APPENDIX

MAJOR DRAMATISTS OF THE WESTERN WORLD

The purpose of this list is to give the reader an outline of the historical development of drama in the theatres of the Western World. It makes no pretense of including all the dramatists, or even all the plays of those mentioned. It does attempt to include representative works of the more significant playwrights.

The plays starred (*) are especially recommended for reading and study by those who are interested in the influence of religion on the drama.

PART I. ANCIENT AND MEDIEVAL DRAMA

I. ANCIENT GREEK DRAMA

Festivals of Dionysus
Aeschylus (Tragedies) (525–456 B.C.)
(Theme of all his plays: Righteousness must be the goal of all human actions—otherwise destruction for society.)
The Suppliants
The Persians
Seven Against Thebes
Agamemnon
The Choephoroe (Libation-Bearers)
The Eumenides
Prometheus Bound

Sophocles (Tragedies) 497–406 B.C.)
   (Highly ethical but more intensely personal and individual than Aeschylus.)
   *Antigone
   Ajax
   *King Oedipus
   Electra
   The Trachinian Maidens
   Philoctetes
   *Oedipus at Colonos
Euripides (Tragedies) (480–406 B.C.)
   (Less religious—more humanistic than Aeschylus and Sophocles.)
   *Electra
   Iphigenia in Tauris
   *Medea
Aristophanes (Comedies) (482–385 B.C.)
   The Frogs
   The Clouds
   Plutus, the God of Riches
Aristotle's Definition of Function of Drama: "To cleanse the passions of fear and pity by an exalted use thereof."

II. ROMAN DRAMA

   Plautus (Comedies) (254?–184 B.C.)
      The Twins
      The Captives
   Terence (Comedies) (190?–159 B.C.)
      Phormio
   Seneca (Tragedies) (4 B.C.–A.D. 65)
      (Rewrote in Latin the Greek tragic stories of Oedipus and Medea and Agamemnon, but without the Greek elevation and feeling, sincerity, and poetry.)
   (Mimes and Pantomimes)

III. HEBREW DRAMA
  *Job (Contemporary with Plays of Ancient Greece)

IV. MEDIEVAL MYSTERIES AND MIRACLES
  Passion Plays
  Saints' Plays
  Mystery Plays (15th and 16th centuries)
    (Cycle of Life and Passion of Christ)
  Miracle Plays
    (Cycle of stories of both Old and New Testaments)
    Old Time Church Drama Adapted (Osgood)
    Harvard Dramatic Club Miracle Plays (Robinson)
    The Second Shepherd's Play, etc. (Child)
  Morality Plays (15th century)
    Everyman
  Interludes
  Masques (Italy and England)
    E.g. "Comus" by John Milton

V. ELIZABETHAN DRAMA
  Marlowe (1564–93)
    Tamburlaine
    The Jew of Malta
    **Dr. Faustus*
  Shakespeare (1564–1616)
    Romeo and Juliet
    Julius Caesar
    **Hamlet*
    **Othello*
    **King Lear*
    Macbeth
    Tempest
  Jonson (1573–1637)
    Everyman in His Humour
    The Alchemist

VI. CONTINENTAL DRAMA

    A. *Spanish*

        Lope De Vega (1562–1635)

          (Left nearly 800 plays—tragedies, farces, comedies, romances. Wove into them the old ballads people loved. Exploited gallantry, often at expense of morality. "Love excuses everything" his motto.)

        The Star of Seville

        Calderon (1600–1681)

          (Soldier and priest. General purpose of his plays: Glorification of Church and king. Added a touch of fantasy and of mysticism.)

        The Devotion of the Cross

        Life Is a Dream

    B. *French*

        Corneille (1606–1684)

        Le Cid

        Polyeucte

        Racine (1639–1699)

        Britannicus

        Iphigenie

        Phèdre

        Esther (Biblical)

        Athalie (Biblical)

        Molière (1622–1673)

          (Real name: Jean Baptiste Poquelin. Greatest French writer of comedy. He exposed and satirized the follies, vices, and affectations of his day. Forerunner of modern drama in this and in his interest in everyday people. Developed in character form the abstractions of the morality plays.)

        Tartuffe (The Hypocrite)

        The Misanthrope

    The Doctor in Spite of Himself
    The Miser
C. *Early German*
    Lessing (1729–1781)
      Miss Sara Sampson
      *Nathan the Wise (Inter-racial drama)
    Goethe (1749–1832)
      Iphigenie
      Egmont
      Torquato Tasso
      Faust (Part I. 1808. Part II. 1827–32)
      Spiritual experience of Goethe—and of Mankind. Immanence of God rather than transcendence. Doctrines of work and service, of inner freedom. The persistent seeking of the Ideal.
    Schiller (1759–1805)
      (Apostle of liberty. Philosophic poet.)
      Wallenstein
      Maria Stuart
      *Wilhelm Tell

PART II.   MODERN DRAMA

VII. Scandinavian Drama (The Theater of Ideas)
    Ibsen (1828–1906) (Norwegian)
    (Leading exponent of drama of Ideas.
    Historic drama had been concerned with human experiences, with story.
    Ibsen's drama was particularly concerned with *why* people did as they did.)
    Three periods:
      Romantic:

Brand
Peer Gynt
Emperor and Galilean
Realistic:
  Comedy of Love
  League of Youth
  Pillars of Society
  An Enemy of the People
  Doll's House
  Ghosts
Symbolic:
  Master Builder
  When We Dead Awaken

Björnson (1832–1910) (Norwegian)
  (Beginning of Social Drama.
  A link between extreme individualism of Ibsen and
  collectivism of later dramatists.)
  The Editor
  The New System
  The Gauntlet
  Beyond Human Power (a study of the effect of faith on
    the human will)

Strindberg (1849–1912) (Swedish)
  (Naturalistic Drama—that is, photographic rather
  than interpretative.
  Sought God; found the devil.
  Five naturalistic sex plays.)
  The Father
  Julie
  Comrades
  Creditors
  The Link

VIII. RUSSIAN DRAMA

Ostrovosky (1823–1886)
(First professional playwright of Russia. Creator of
Realistic Russian Theatre. 48 plays. Discarded ancient
ideas of expiation of guilt, of good-evil conflict, of
villains and heroes. Left problems unsolved.)
It's a Family Affair
The Storm

Turgenev (1818–1883)
(Known chiefly as a novelist, but left five comedies.
Had profound influence in freeing serfs.)

Tolstoy (1828–1910)
(Novelist, Dramatist, Educator, Social Reformer,
Seeker after God.)
Two great plays:
   *Power of Darkness (Theme: Power of evil to coil
      itself about one until escape is impossible except
      by divine forgiveness.)
The Living Corpse (or Redemption)

Tchekov (or Chekhov) (1860–1904)
(A physician with a philanthropic disposition. Investi-
gated penal institutions. "The dramatist of despond-
ency.")
The Three Sisters
*Uncle Vanya
The Cherry Orchard

Gorky (1868–1936) Real name: Alexi Pyeshkoff.
(Drama of the disinherited. Culmination of drama of
naturalism.)
*The Lower Depths (or *At the Bottom*)
   A study of the dregs of life. A spark of divinity in
   each; it flares up for a moment, then dies.

Andreyev (1871–1919)
(Drama of Human Destiny)
"Man refuses to be a failure, although death ends a
life which has not revealed its meaning." (Miller)
To the Stars
*The Life of Man
He Who Gets Slapped

IX. MODERN FRENCH DRAMA

Bacque (1837–1899)
(Founder of realistic school of drama in France)
The Vultures (Les Corbeaux)
The Merry-Go-Round

Brieux (1858–1932)
(Social reformer through drama. Thesis plays.)
Maternity (Theme: The social need of birth control.)
Damaged Goods (Theme: Denunciation of the igno-
rance surrounding social disease.)
The Three Daughters of Monsieur Du Pont (Theme:
Arraignment of marriage of convenience.)
The Red Robe (Theme: The French system of crimi-
nal justice needs reform.)

Hervieu (1857–1915)
(Drama of Moral Ideas)
Know Thyself
The Passing of the Torch

Maeterlinck (1862–1939)
(Belgian by birth. Poet, mystic, philosopher, essayist,
dramatist. Return to Romanticism.)
Pelleas and Melisande
The Blue Bird
The Betrothal
Mary Magdalene

Rostand (1868–1918)
(Romanticist, yet influenced strongly by naturalism.)
L'Aiglon
Chantecler
Cyrano de Bergerac

X. MODERN GERMAN DRAMA

Sudermann (1857–1928)
(Drama of compromise between realism and romanticism.)
Magda
The Fires of St. John
The Joy of Living
The Vale of Content

Hauptmann (1862–1934)
(Naturalism and social drama in Germany reached their culmination in him.)
The Weavers (Social drama. Theme: the dire social effect of hunger.)
Drayman Henschel (Theme: Slow disintegration of character under a sense of guilt and of terror of the supernatural.)
*Rose Brand
The Rats

Schnitzler (1862–1931)
(Drama of Disillusionment. A Jewish physician.)
The Living Hours
The Lonely Way

XI. MODERN ENGLISH DRAMA

Thomas Hardy (1840–1928)
The Dynasts (poetic drama of Napoleonic era)

Henry Arthur Jones (1851–1929)
  The Case of Rebellious Susan (Double Standard)
  Michael and His Lost Angel (Reaction of a secret sin
    upon a priest)
  Judah (Religious zeal and faith-healing)
  Mrs. Dane's Defense
  Mary Goes First

Arthur Wing Pinero (1855–1935)
  *The Second Mrs. Tanqueray
  The Notorious Mrs. Ebbsmith
  The Thunderbolt
  *Midchannel

George Bernard Shaw (1856–   )
  (A satirical philosopher attacking poverty and war and
  championing freedom from every form of tyranny)
  Widowers' Houses
  Arms and the Man
  Candida
  The Devil's Disciple
  Caesar and Cleopatra
  Man and Superman
  Major Barbara
  The Doctor's Dilemma
  *Androcles and the Lion
  Pygmalion
  Back to Methuselah
  *Saint Joan

J. M. Barrie (1860–1937)
  (Drama of fantasy and whimsy)
  Quality Street
  The Admirable Crichton
  Alice-Sit-by-the-Fire
  What Every Woman Knows

Peter Pan
A Kiss for Cinderella
*Dear Brutus
The Old Lady Shows Her Medals
Mary Rose
The Twelve Pound Look
Israel Zangwill (1864–1926)
  (Social Drama)
  *The Melting Pot
  The War God
John Galsworthy (1867–1933)
  (Drama of Social Injustice)
  *Strife (Capital and labor)
  Justice (Prison reform)
  *Loyalties (Lesser loyalties must be subordinated to loyalty to mankind)
  The Skin Game
Stephen Phillips (1868–1915)
  (Revived Poetic Drama)
  *Paola and Francesca
  Herod
  The Sin of David
  Nero
Granville Barker (1877–1946)
  The Voysey Inheritance
  The Madras House
  The Secret Life
John Masefield (1878–   )
  The Tragedy of Nan
  *The Coming of Christ
  Good Friday
  Easter
  *The Trial of Jesus

John Drinkwater (1882–1937)
X = O: A Night of the Trojan War
The Storm
Abraham Lincoln
Robert E. Lee
Oliver Cromwell
Mary Stuart

A. A. Milne (1882–   )
Mr. Pim Passes By
The Dover Road

Sutton Vane (1888–   )
*Outward Bound

Thomas Stearns Eliot (1888–   )
The Rock
*Murder in the Cathedral
The Family Reunion

Benn Levy (1900–   )
Mrs. Moonlight
*Art and Mrs. Bottle
*The Devil Passes

Emlyn Williams (1905–   )
Night Must Fall
Morning Star
Light of Heart
He Was Born Gay
*The Corn Is Green

XII. MODERN IRISH DRAMA

Lady Gregory (1859–1932)
Folk-History Plays
Seven Short Plays

William Butler Yeats (1865–1939)
  The Land of Heart's Desire
  *The Hour Glass

Lord Dunsany (1878–   )
  The Gods of the Mountain
  Plays of Gods and Men
  If
  Plays of the Near and Far

St. John Ervine (1883–   )
  Mixed Marriage (Study of religious tolerance)
  Jane Cleg
  John Ferguson

Sean O'Casey (1884–   )
  Juno and the Paycock
  Within the Gates

Lennox Robinson (1886–   )
  (Contemporary folk-drama)
  The White-Headed Boy
  The Far-Off Hills

Paul Vincent Carroll (1900–   )
  Shadow and Substance
  The White Steed

XIII. MODERN SPANISH DRAMA

Jose Echegaray (1833–1916)
  The Great Galeoto (Theme: Power of false suggestion
    to create the guilt which it suspects.)
  Madman or Saint?
  The World and His Wife

Jacinto Benavente (1866–   )
  The Bonds of Interest

   Mary the Third
   When Ladies Meet
   *Susan and God

Channing Pollock (1880–1946)
   The Fool
   *The Enemy
   Mr. Moneypenny
   The House Beautiful

Walter Ferris (1882–   )
   *Death Takes a Holiday

Martin Flavin (1883–   )
   Children of the Moon
   *The Criminal Code
   Crossroads
   Broken Dishes
   *Amaco
   Sunday

Hatcher Hughes (1886–   )
   A Marriage Made in Heaven
   Hell-Bent for Heaven

Percival Wilde (1887–   )
   Mothers of Men
   One-Act Plays (First Series, 1933)
   One-Act Plays (Second Series, 1934)

Eugene O'Neill (1888–   )
   The Emperor Jones
   The Hairy Ape
   All God's Chillun Got Wings
   The Great God Brown
   Lazarus Laughed
   Strange Interlude
   *Mourning Becomes Electra
   *Days Without End

Maxwell Anderson (1888–   )
   Saturday's Children
   *Winterset
   Elizabeth the Queen
   Night Over Taos
   Mary of Scotland
   *Both Your Houses
   *Valley Forge
   The Wingless Victory
   High Tor
   *Journey to Jerusalem
   *Joan of Lorraine
Marc Connelly (1890–   )
   *The Wisdom Tooth
   *The Green Pastures
Sidney Howard (1891–1939)
   They Knew What They Wanted
   *The Silver Cord
   Yellowjack
   *Alien Corn
Elmer Rice (1892–   )
   The Adding Machine
   *Street Scene
   Counselor at Law
   Judgment Day
   Dream Girl
Samuel Nathaniel Behrman (1893–   )
   The Second Man
   Biography
   Rain from Heaven
   End of Summer
Paul Green (1894–   )
   The Lord's Will

*In Abraham's Bosom
The House of Connelly
The Southern Cross
Hymn to the Rising Sun*

Philip Barry (1896–   )
  *You and I
  *John
  Holiday
  Tomorrow and Tomorrow
  The Joyous Season
  Here Come the Clowns*

Robert Emmet Sherwood (1896–   )
  *The Road to Rome
  Idiot's Delight
  Abe Lincoln in Illinois
  There Shall Be No Night*

Thornton Wilder (1897–   )
  The Angel That Troubled the Waters
    (One-act plays)
  *Our Town
  The Skin of Our Teeth

Emmet Lavery (1901–   )
  *The First Legion
  Yankee From Olympus*

Clifford Odets (1901–   )
  *Awake and Sing
  Paradise Lost
  Golden Boy
  Rocket to the Moon
  Waiting for Lefty* (one-act)

Lillian Hellman (1904–   )
  *The Children's Hour
  The Little Foxes*

Days to Come
Watch on the Rhine
The Searching Wind

Sidney Kingsley (1906–   )
Men in White
Dead End
The Patriots

Leopold Atlas (1908–   )
Wednesday's Child
The House We Live In

William Saroyan (1908–   )
My Heart's in the Highlands
The Time of Your Life
The Beautiful People

Irwin Shaw (1912–   )
Bury the Dead
The Gentle People

XVII. CONTEMPORARY ONE-ACT RELIGIOUS DRAMAS, suitable
for use by church drama groups. The reader may secure
without charge a printed pamphlet, "A Selected List
of Religious Dramas," upon request to the Drama
Office of the Chicago Theological Seminary, 5757
University Avenue, Chicago 37.

BOOKS USED IN PREPARATION OF THE FOREGOING LIST

Haigh, A. E. *The Tragic Drama of the Greeks.* Thorough. Especially good for lives of Aeschylus, Sophocles, and Euripides.

Haigh, A. E. *The Attic Theatre.* Thorough treatment of Greek Theatre.

Mantzius, Karl. *A History of Theatrical Art.* 6 Vols. (Parts of Vols. 1 and 2 for Greek, Roman, and Medieval Plays and for brief accounts of Chinese, Japanese, and Indian theatres.)

Knowlton, Edgar C. *An Outline of World Literature.*

Taylor, Joseph Richard. *The Story of the Drama.* A popular account. See especially the sections on Greek and Medieval drama.

Murray, Gilbert. *Fifteen Greek Plays.* Introduction contains a short historical account.

Nicoll, Allardyce. *British Drama.* Historical survey from the beginnings to 1925.

Matthews, Brander. *The Development of the Drama.* (For brief sketches of Greek tragedy and Medieval drama.)

Gassner, John. *Masters of the Drama.* A comprehensive historical and critical study of the drama from primitive times to our own day.

Clark, Barrett H. *A Study of the Modern Drama.* Survey of Drama in Europe and America in Nineteenth and Twentieth Centuries.

Miller, Nellie Burget. *The Living Drama.* An outline with study notes of the history of drama in the western world.

Cheney, Sheldon. *The Theatre.* Historical survey of 3000 years of the theatre.

Bates, Katherine. *The English Religious Drama.* A short scholarly work.

Robinson, D. F. *The Harvard Dramatic Club Miracle Plays.* Several of the Medieval plays translated and adapted.

Osgood, P. E. *Old-Time Church Drama Adapted.* A few of the Medieval plays adapted for present-day use.

Baldwin, T. W. *Earlier English Drama.* For Medieval religious drama.

Drew, Elizabeth. *Discovering Drama.* A discussion of the relationship between the theatre and literature.